NURSERY

R · H · Y · M · E · S

in
CROSS STITCH

NURSERY
R · H · Y · M · E · S

in
CROSS STITCH

Dorothea Hall

MEREHURST

ACKNOWLEDGEMENTS

The author would like to offer her grateful thanks to the following people who helped with the cross stitching of projects in this book with such skill and enthusiasm: Gisela Banbury, Clarice Blakey, Caroline Davies, Christina Eustace, Janet Grey, Elizabeth Hall and Anne Whitbourn.

The publishers would like to thank Julie Hasler for her designs on pages 16-17, 24-25, 28-29, 36-37, 42-50, 53, 56-61, 64-65, 68, 72, 76, 84, 88 and 112-117, and for her help with the designs on pages 12-13, 33, 78-79, 92-93 and 96-97.

The publishers would also like to thank The Monogrammed Linen Shop, 68 Walton Street, London SW3, and Thomas Goode & Co, 19 South Audley Street, London W1Y 6BN, for kindly supplying linen and china on pages 34 and 110.

Published 1991 by Merehurst Limited
Ferry House, 51-57 Lacy Road, Putney, London SW15 1PR

© Copyright 1991 Merehurst Limited
ISBN 1 85391 162 3 (Cased)

A catalogue record for this book is available from the British Library.

Project Editor: Polly Boyd
Edited by Diana Brinton
Designed by Maggie Aldred
Photography by Di Lewis (pages 34-35, 110-111 by Stewart Grant)
Illustrations by John Hutchinson
Typesetting by Maron Graphics Limited
Colour separation by Fotographics Limited, London – Hong Kong
Printed in Italy by New Interlitho, S.p.A., Milan

Merehurst is the leading publisher of craft books and has an excellent range of titles to suit all levels. Please send to the address above for our free catalogue, stating the title of this book.

CONTENTS

ℐNTRODUCTION

The tremendous feeling of satisfaction and pleasure we experience in embroidering and making a project – whether it is a quilt for the nursery or a simple bookmark for a friend – is borne out by the growing enthusiasm for cross stitch and the general revival of interest in traditional domestic crafts. The projects in this book, all of which are based on old nursery rhymes, include some which are suitable for beginners as well as others that are more challenging and are designed for experienced embroiderers.

Some of the most striking illustrations, and the most adaptable for cross stitch embroidery, are those of R. Caldecott, whose sensitive line and use of flat, subtle colour is clearly inspirational.

Not all nursery rhyme designs need be of large proportions – indeed, the smallest motifs can be equally charming (and much quicker to embroider), as seen here in the lavender sachets and the Little Boy Blue pillow cover.

Cross stitch occupies a special place among embroidery crafts, for it was at one time a much-practised activity. Young girls were taught to embroider by working immensely detailed samplers in cross stitch, learning to embroider all kinds of complex designs, repeating border patterns, letters and numerals with great dexterity and charm, before progressing to other household items, such as hand-towels, napkins, table-cloths and pillow covers.

While researching nursery rhymes for this book, I have found a similar charm and variety in the beautifully illustrated verses handed down from past generations. In fact, charm played a major part in the inspiration of the book, since so much came initially from the nursery rhymes themselves and from the equally delightful illustrations. What child, for example, could resist the magic of 'Hey, diddle diddle, the cat and the fiddle, the cow jumped over the moon', and what mother would not respond to 'Little maiden, better tarry; time enough next year to marry'. Evocative verses such as these, combined with the artistry of A. Rackham and R. Caldecott, for example, have kept me thoroughly inspired and amused from beginning to end.

The choice of projects proved tantalizing, as did matching a particular nursery rhyme to a project. However, it would be a simple operation to convert many of the designs to suit your personal needs. Take the miniature pictures, for example, or the traditional dressing table set; these designs could quite easily be mounted as greetings cards or pincushions. And the tray designs could equally well be used as pictures or cushion covers. The child's patchwork quilt, embroidered with verses of twelve popular nursery rhymes, is in itself a miniature record of some of our best-loved verses. And what would make handier bed-time reading? Indeed the quilt might even become a teaching aid to encourage reading skills! As an alternative to a quilt, however, you may prefer to embroider the verses (or any of the other verses given in the book) and stitch them together to make a washable fabric book. With a little pre-planning, you could have immense fun adding borders of your choice, or using some of those given at the end of the book, to create further designs of your own. Using the alphabet, also given at the end of the book, you can add initials to your embroidery or spell out a name to personalize your gifts. The combinations are endless.

If, in making these projects, you experience the satisfaction and fun I have had in creating them; this will happen because cross stitch and our well-loved nursery rhymes have an enduring attraction and, hopefully, will continue to be cherished by generations to come.

BEFORE YOU BEGIN

Each project begins with a full list of the materials that you will require. Note that the measurements given for the embroidery fabric include a minimum of 3cm (1¼in) all around to allow for stretching it in a frame and preparing the edges.

A colour key for DMC stranded embroidery cotton is given with each chart. You will need to buy one skein of each colour mentioned, though you may use less. Where two or more skeins are needed this is mentioned in the main list of requirements. Each cross stitch colour is represented by a symbol, but backstitch (bks) colours are listed by number only. Where a backstitch number is followed by a star, you will need to buy that colour in addition to the others. All other backstitch colours are also used for cross stitching and will therefore be mentioned in the list against a symbol.

Should you wish to use Coats/Anchor or Madeira stranded embroidery cottons, refer to the conversion chart given at the back of the book.

To work from the charts, particularly those where several symbols are used in close proximity, some readers may find it helpful to have the chart enlarged so that the squares and symbols can be seen more easily. Many photocopying services will do this for a minimum charge.

When you begin to cross stitch, use the centre lines given on the chart and the basting threads on your fabric as reference points for counting the squares and threads to position your design accurately.

DRINKS TRAY

When friends come to stay, what better way is there to say 'good night' than to share a bed-time drink on a tray you've embroidered yourself?

❖

COME OUT TO PLAY

Girls and boys come out to play,
The moon doth shine as bright as day;
Leave your supper, and leave your sleep,
And come with your playfellows into
the street.
Come with a whoop, come with a call,
Come with a good will or not at all.

COME OUT TO PLAY ▲

☻ white (bks 926)
÷ 832 gold
↑ 225 flesh (bks 3354)
✳ 3354 pink

● 3350 deep pink
= 598 blue (bks 926)
◆ 733 olive
↓ 731 dark olive
S 422 buff

⊡ 831 brown
I 926 grey blue
◣ 924 dark grey blue
○ 3024 light grey (bks 535)
△ 535 dark grey

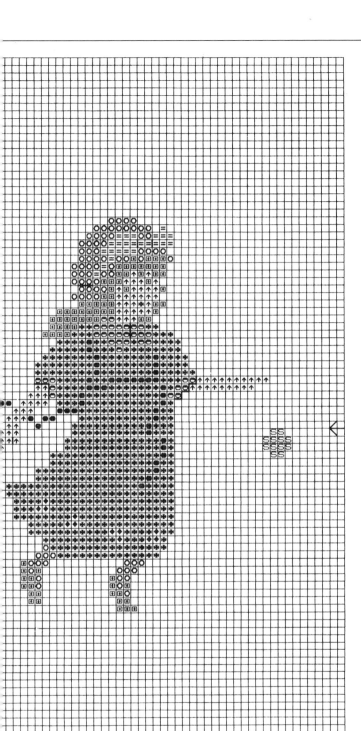

DRINKS TRAY

YOU WILL NEED

For a tray measuring 33cm × 20.5cm
(13in × 8in) with a 28.5cm × 16cm
(11¼in × 6¼in) oval cut out:

*40cm × 30cm (16in × 12in) of cream evenweave
(Aida) fabric, 14 threads to 2.5cm (1in)
DMC stranded embroidery cotton in the colours
given in the panel shown opposite
No24 tapestry needle
33cm × 20.5cm (13in × 8in) of lightweight
iron-on interfacing
Oval wooden tray (for suppliers, see page 128)*

•

THE EMBROIDERY

Begin by stretching the prepared fabric in an embroidery frame (see page 121). Then, following the colour key and chart, complete the cross stitching, using two strands of thread in the needle throughout. Remove the embroidery from the frame and, if necessary, steam press it on the wrong side. Do not remove the basting stitches at this stage.

ASSEMBLING THE TRAY

Using a soft pencil, mark the mounting card (supplied with the tray) both ways along the centre.

Lay the embroidery face down on a clean surface. Centre the card over it, with the pencil lines and basting stitches matching, and lightly draw around the card outline, using the pencil. Remove the basting threads, carefully cut out the embroidery, and back it with the lightweight iron-on interfacing. Alternatively, trim the fabric to leave a 4cm (1½in) allowance, and run a gathering thread around 12mm (½in) away from the pencil line. Position the card and pull up the gathers evenly. Either lace across the back or secure the edges with masking tape.

Follow the manufacturer's instructions to complete the assembly of your tray.

NIGHTDRESS CASE

Make this roomy bag to tuck away your nightie or pyjamas for the day. It is lightly padded and finished with bows, and will sit comfortably on top of the bed, as soft as any pillow.

✦ ◆ ✦

BAA-BAA BLACK SHEEP

Baa-baa black sheep, have you any wool?
Yes sir, yes sir, three bags full;
One for my master, one for my dame,
And one for the little boy who lives in
our lane.

BAA-BAA BLACK SHEEP ▲

H white (bks 415)

✕ 744 yellow

⊖ 742 orange	‖ 948 flesh (bks 352)	◣ 3053 sap green
△ 729 gold	↑ 3325 blue	÷ 470 green
↓ 434 brown	⊡ 322 dark blue	◆ 935 dark green
✱ 352 pink	= 471 light green	S 415 light grey

△ 317 grey
● 310 black

NIGHTDRESS CASE

YOU WILL NEED

For a nightdress case measuring 41cm × 30·5cm (16in × 12in):

90cm × 46cm (1yd × 18in) of dusky pink evenweave fabric such as Lugana 403, 25 threads to 2.5cm (1in)
90cm × 46cm (1yd × 18in) of pale pink lawn for the lining
90cm × 46cm (1yd × 18in) of lightweight synthetic batting
115cm (1¼yds) of matching pink ribbon, 2cm (¾in) wide
DMC stranded embroidery cotton in the colours given in the panel on page 16
No26 tapestry needle
Matching sewing thread

•

THE EMBROIDERY

With the edges prepared, stretch the top fabric in an embroidery frame, see page 121. Baste the fold lines as shown in the diagram, and baste the positioning lines for the motif, following the chart given opposite. Then, referring to the colour key and the chart, complete the cross stitching, using two strands of thread in the needle throughout; use a single strand for the backstitching. Remove the fabric from the frame and steam press on the wrong side, if necessary.

MAKING THE NIGHTDRESS CASE

Place the top fabric face down on a flat surface; carefully smooth the batting on top, and pin and baste. Trim the edges of the batting to clear the seam allowance all around and catch-stitch the edges of the batting to the seam allowance.

Make a single turning on the short edge (not the flap edge) of the front section and baste; 12mm (½in) seam allowances are used throughout. With right sides facing, fold up the front section, baste and machine stitch the side seams to form the pocket. Trim the corners and turn to the right side.

Make a single turning on the short edge of the

lining fabric and repeat as for the top fabric, but do not turn the pocket to the right side.

With right sides of the top fabric and lining together, baste and stitch around the flap, finishing just above the side seams. Trim the corners and turn the flap through to the right side. Slip the lining into the pocket and slipstitch the top edges together, easing the turning so that the stitching is on the inside. Remove the basting stitches.

Cut the ribbon into two equal lengths. Make two bows and catch-stitch them to the flap edge, as shown on the diagram.

CUTTING LAYOUT

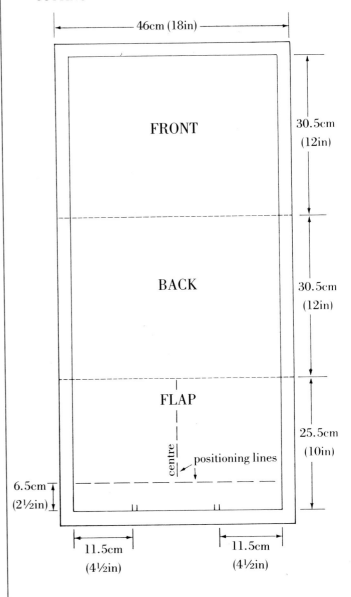

*L*ACY LAVENDER SACHETS

These sweet-smelling sachets
will become favourite gifts
for family and friends.

MARY, MARY, QUITE CONTRARY

Mary, Mary, quite contrary,
How does your garden grow?
With silver bells and cockle-shells,
And pretty maids all in a row.

•

LAVENDER BLUE

Lavender's blue, dilly dilly,
lavender's green,
When I am king, dilly dilly,
you shall be queen.

•

BUTTERFLY, BUTTERFLY

Butterfly, butterfly, whence do you come?
I know not, I ask not, I never had a home.

•

THE ROSE IS RED

The rose is red, the violet blue,
The gilly flower sweet – and so are you.

LACY LAVENDER SACHETS

YOU WILL NEED

For one sachet, with an overall measurement of 23cm × 15cm (9in × 6in):

50cm × 20cm (20in × 8in) of white openweave fabric, such as cotton Davosa or natural linen, 18 threads to 2.5cm (1in)
32.5cm (13in) of pre-gathered white lace trim, 4cm (1½in) wide
70cm (28in) of double-sided white satin ribbon, 1cm (⅜in) wide
DMC stranded embroidery cotton in the colours given in the appropriate panel on pages 20, 21
No26 tapestry needle
Matching sewing thread
Sufficient lavender or pot pourri to fill the sachet halfway

•

THE EMBROIDERY

To transfer the positioning lines to the embroidery, fold the fabric widthways in half and mark this line with a pin. Measure 8cm (3in) in from this point and baste across. Baste the upright centre line.

With the fabric held in a hoop, follow the chart and complete the motif, using two strands of thread in the needle. Where several colours are required, and to save time in starting and finishing, you may prefer to keep two or three needles in use, pinning them to the side when those particular colours are not being used.

Remove the basting stitches and steam press the finished embroidery on the wrong side.

MAKING UP THE SACHET

With the wrong side facing out, fold the fabric widthways in half; baste and machine stitch the sides, taking a 2.5cm (1in) seam. If the edges have frayed, check that the width of the sachet is 15cm (6in). Trim the seam allowances to 12mm (½in), and turn to the right side. Make a 4cm (1½in) single turning on the top edge and baste.

Join the short edges of the lace trim, using a tiny french seam. Pin and baste the trim to the inside of the top edge and, working from the right side, machine stitch in place, sewing close to the top edge.

Half fill the sachet with lavender and tie the ribbon twice around the top, finishing with the bow in front.

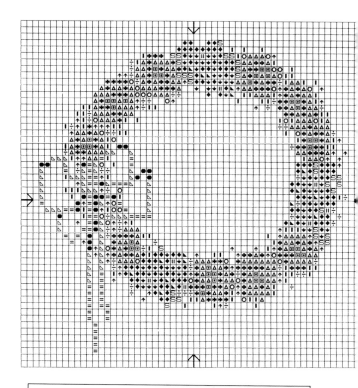

THE ROSE IS RED ▲

‖ 445 yellow	✦ 792 violet
△ 3733 pink	= 3761 turquoise
✱ 603 magenta	÷ 959 veridian green
⊡ 817 dark red	⊃ 943 dark green
◆ 341 pale blue	┃ 989 green
◺ 794 blue	↑ 471 olive
● 798 deep blue	○ 3051 dark olive
◣ 3609 mauve	

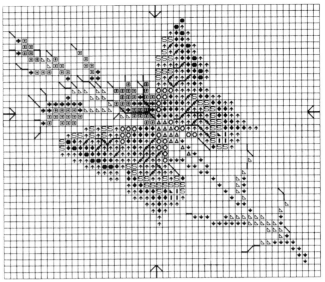

BUTTERFLY, BUTTERFLY ▲

↑ 445 yellow
◣ 783 ochre
Ɩ 721 orange
◆ 734 khaki (bks wing)
⊡ 602 pink
✚ 349 red

△ 989 green
↓ 993 veridian green
○ 930 dark green blue
S 340 light blue
● 792 dark blue
△ 824 navy blue

MARY, MARY ▲

Ɩɩ white (bks bloomers 930,
      collar 794)
◇ 745 pale lemon
      (bks butterfly wing 783)
✕ 445 pale yellow
◺ 444 bright yellow
◆ 783 deep yellow
↑ 948 flesh (bks cockle shells 783)
⊡ 605 pink
● 603 deep pink
✚ 3705 red
= 3761 pale blue
⬭ 3766 turquoise
↓ 930 slate grey (bks butterfly body)
Ɩ 794 blue
S 564 pale green
△ 958 veridian green
÷ 3348 green
◣ 702 dark green
○ 3053 khaki

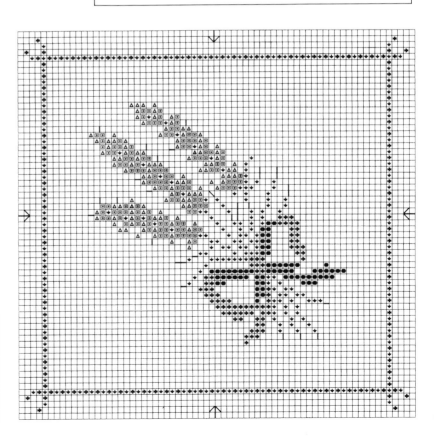

LAVENDER BLUE ▶

✚ 224 pink   △ 341 blue
● 892 geranium   ↓ 368 green
⊡ 340 violet   (bks stems)

FRINGED PLACE MATS AND NAPKINS

Breakfast for two! Give a little personal touch to plain place mats and napkins by embroidering them with these exquisite corner motifs and finishing with a simple fringed hem.

HICKETY, PICKETY

Hickety, pickety, my black hen,
She lays eggs for gentlemen;
Gentlemen come every day
To see what my black hen doth lay.

•

HUMPTY DUMPTY

Humpty Dumpty sat on a wall
Humpty Dumpty had a great fall;
All the King's horses and all the King's men
Couldn't put Humpty Dumpty together again.

FRINGED PLACE MATS AND NAPKINS

YOU WILL NEED

For two place mats, each measuring
47cm × 33cm (18½in × 13in), and two napkins
each measuring 40.5cm (16in) square:

*90cm (1yd) of evenweave (Linda) fabric
84cm (33in) wide, 27 threads to 2.5cm (1in);
alternatively, prepared table mats can be purchased
from specialist suppliers (see page 128)
DMC stranded embroidery cotton in the colours
given in the panels
No26 tapestry needle
Matching sewing threads*

THE EMBROIDERY

Cut out the mats and napkins, following the cutting layout shown opposite. The finished fringed edge should be even, so cut straight along the grain.

Following the chart, baste the positioning lines at the bottom right of the fabric, 4cm (1½in) in from both sides. With the fabric stretched in a hoop, complete the embroidery stitching with a single strand of thread. Remove the basting stitches and steam press on the wrong side.

THE HEM

For the fringed hem, remove a single thread 12mm (½in) in from the outer edge on all four sides. Using matching sewing thread and a round-ended needle, work a single row of hem stitching, taking two threads for each stitch (see page 125). Finally, remove the fabric threads below the hemstitching to complete the fringed edge.

HICKETY, PICKETY ▶

◆ white (bks 453)	⊡ 3328 red
✱ 977 yellow	△ 413 grey
○ 676 gold	● 310 black

CUTTING
LAYOUT

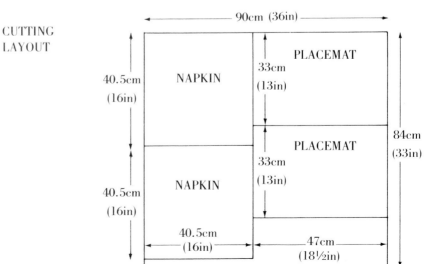

CORDED CUSHION

This charming cushion, embroidered in minute detail and edged with a contrast twisted cord, is the ideal accessory for a favourite armchair or sofa.

❖

I HAD A LITTLE NUT TREE

I had a little nut tree, nothing would it bear
But a silver nutmeg and a golden pear.
The King of Spain's daughter came to visit me,
And all because of my little nut tree.
I skipped over water, I danced over sea,
And all the birds in the air couldn't catch me.

I HAD A LITTLE NUT TREE ▲

↑ ecru (and bks 642*)	○ 977 orange (and bks 975*)	⊐ 3364 soft green	◤ 800 blue (and bks 798*)
I silver (bks 645)	= 948 flesh (bks 352)	(and bks 935*)	⊡ 869 brown
◺ gold thread (bks 610)	● 352 pink	◆ 368 green	↓ 611 drab brown (and bks 938*)

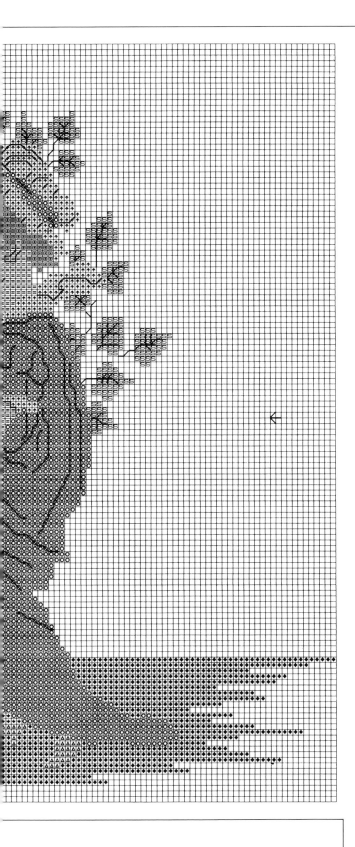

✱ 610 dark drab brown
(bks branches)
△ 645 dark grey

*Note: 5 additional
backstitch colours.*

CORDED CUSHION

YOU WILL NEED

For a cushion cover measuring 39.5cm × 33cm
(15½in × 13in):

*44.5cm × 38cm (17½in × 15in) of ecru
evenweave (Aida) fabric, 14 threads to 2.5cm (1in)
42cm × 35.5cm (16½in × 14in) of either
matching or contrasting backing fabric; 12mm
(½in) seam allowances are included.
1.80m (2yds) of contrast cord, 1cm (⅜in)
in diameter
DMC stranded embroidery cotton in the colours
given in the panel
No24 tapestry needle
Matching sewing threads
42cm × 35.5cm (16½in × 14in) cushion pad*

•

THE EMBROIDERY

Following the instructions on page 121, prepare
your embroidery fabric with basted centre lines and
stretch it in a frame, ready for cross stitching.

Using two strands of thread in the needle, and
following the chart, complete the design.

To achieve this particularly delicate effect, work
all the backstitch lines with a single strand of
thread.

Remove the embroidery from the frame and
lightly steam press on the wrong side.

MAKING THE CUSHION COVER

Using the basting stitches as a guide, trim the edges
evenly, so that the embroidery measures the
same as the backing fabric, 42cm × 35.5cm
(16½in × 14in).

With right sides of the two sections together,
baste and machine stitch around the edges, leaving
a 20cm (8in) opening in the middle of one side.
Remove all the basting stitches; trim across the
corners, and turn the cover to the right side. Insert
the cushion pad; turn in the edges of the opening,
and slipstitch to close.

Finally, attach the cord around the edges, following the instructions on page 124.

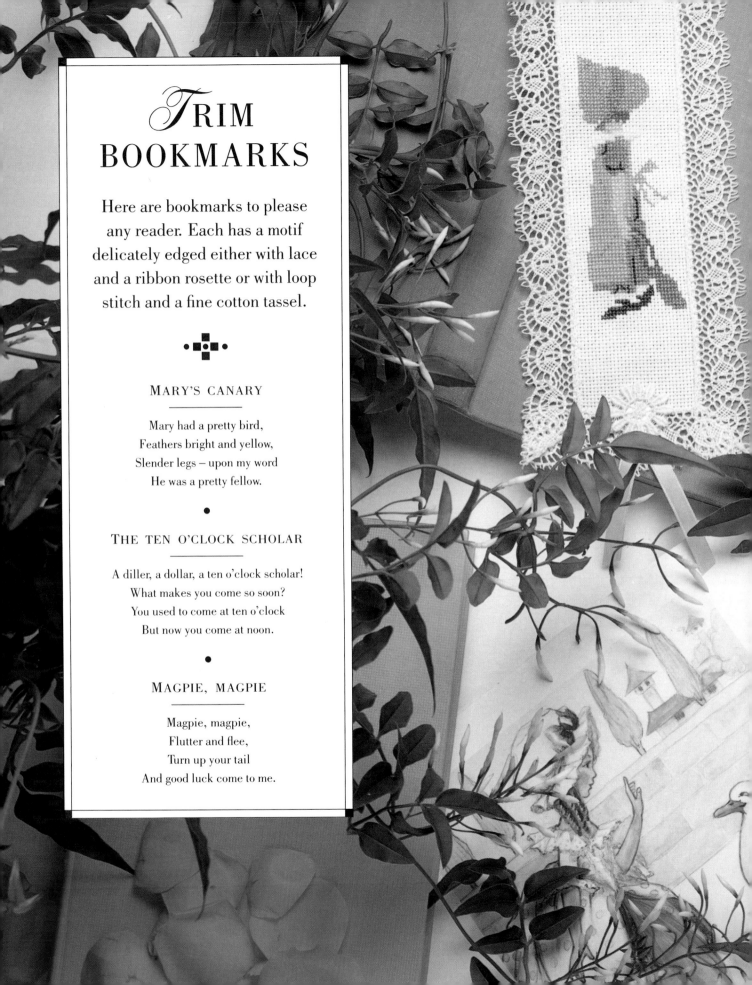

TRIM BOOKMARKS

Here are bookmarks to please any reader. Each has a motif delicately edged either with lace and a ribbon rosette or with loop stitch and a fine cotton tassel.

MARY'S CANARY

Mary had a pretty bird,
Feathers bright and yellow,
Slender legs – upon my word
He was a pretty fellow.

THE TEN O'CLOCK SCHOLAR

A diller, a dollar, a ten o'clock scholar!
What makes you come so soon?
You used to come at ten o'clock
But now you come at noon.

MAGPIE, MAGPIE

Magpie, magpie,
Flutter and flee,
Turn up your tail
And good luck come to me.

TRIM BOOKMARKS

YOU WILL NEED

For the *Mary's Canary* and *The Ten O'clock Scholar* bookmarks, each measuring about 25cm (10in) long:

One cream and one white prepared lace-edged bookmark, 18 threads to 2.5cm (1in), each bookmark 5cm (2in) wide (for suppliers, see page 128)
DMC stranded embroidery cotton in the colours given in the appropriate panel
No26 tapestry needle

For the *Magpie, Magpie* bookmark, also about 25cm (10in) long:

23cm (9in) of white evenweave prepared braid, 5cm (2in) wide, 15 threads to 2.5cm (1in)
DMC stranded embroidery cotton in the colours given in the appropriate panels
No24 tapestry needle
Matching sewing thread

●

THE EMBROIDERY

Working in an embroidery hoop (see page 121 for the instructions on how to stretch small pieces of fabric in a frame) and with basted centre lines, complete the embroidery, using two strands of thread in the needle throughout.

Remove the basting stitches and, if needed, steam press on the wrong side.

FINISHING THE MAGPIE BOOKMARK

Make a small double turning on the top edge and, with matching thread, hem in place.

To make a point on the lower edge, fold the bookmark lengthways in half with the wrong side facing out and backstitch the short edges together. Trim the corner, press the seam open and turn to the right side. Flatten out the bookmark, thus creating a point. Press on the wrong side, and slipstitch to hold.

Make the tassel by winding ordinary white

basting thread around a piece of card about 3cm (1¼in) wide. Thread the end into a needle, slip off the tassel threads and bind the loose thread several times around the bunch, close to the top. Pass the needle up through the binding so that it comes out at the top of the tassel – ready to be sewn to the point.

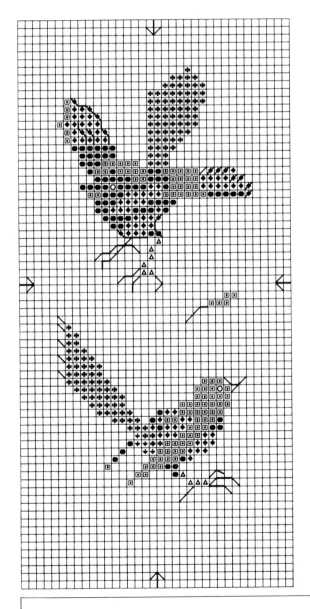

MAGPIE, MAGPIE ▲	
◆ white (bks wings 312, body 823)	⊡ 312 blue
	● 823 dark blue
○ 472 gold	△ 3052 olive (bks feet)
	↓ 937 green
	✱ 904 dark green

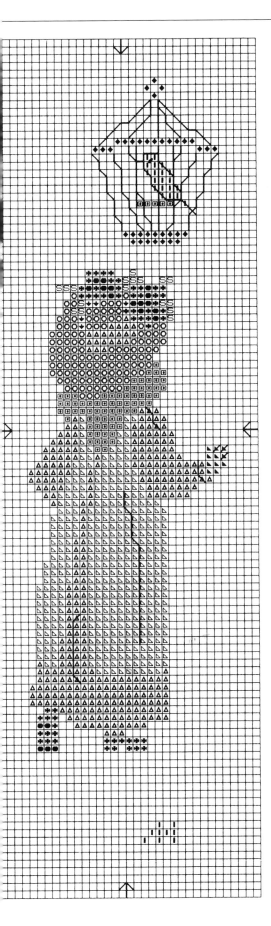

MARY'S CANARY ◄

- ◣ 948 flesh (bks 3326)
- I 445 pale yellow
- ◿ 727 yellow (bks 833)
- ✦ 783 orange
- ○ 833 ochre
- ✱ 3326 pink
- ● 335 deep pink
- △ 794 blue (bks 988)
- S 913 green
- ◆ 988 dark green
- ⊡ 3011 dark brown

TEN O'CLOCK SCHOLAR ►

- ◣ white (and bks 415*)
- I 948 flesh
- ✱ 968 pink (bks 3766)
- ○ 3766 sea green (bks 931)
- ● 931 deep blue green
- ◆ 738 straw
- ✦ 435 brown
- △ 612 drab brown
- ⊡ 611 dark brown

*Note: one additional backstitch colour**

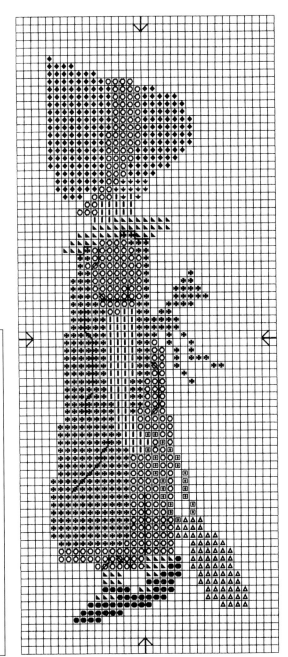

TEA-TIME TRAY

When guests call for tea,
enchant them with this delightful
tray – beautifully embroidered
and mounted under glass.

◆

A FROG HE WOULD A-
WOOING GO

———

A frog, he would a-wooing go,
Heigho! says Rowley,
Whether his mother would let him or no,
With a rowley, powley, gammon and spinach,
Heigho! says Anthony Rowley.

A FROG HE WOULD A-WOOING GO ▲

6 white	⊟ 3325 pale blue	△ 830 drab brown
L 727 yellow	I 312 dark blue	↓ 613 stone (and bks 611*)
◇ gold thread	A 734 light olive	T 415 pale grey
÷ 676 gold	(and bks 730*)	= 414 steel grey (bks 310)
◣ 680 deep gold	‖ 523 green	◤ 317 dark grey
H 754 pale pink	◆ 367 dark green	● 310 black (bks 317)
(bks 352)	↑ 520 dark drab green	*Note: 2 additional*
⊡ 758 pink	S 435 light brown	*backstitch colours*
✱ 355 red	○ 832 golden brown	

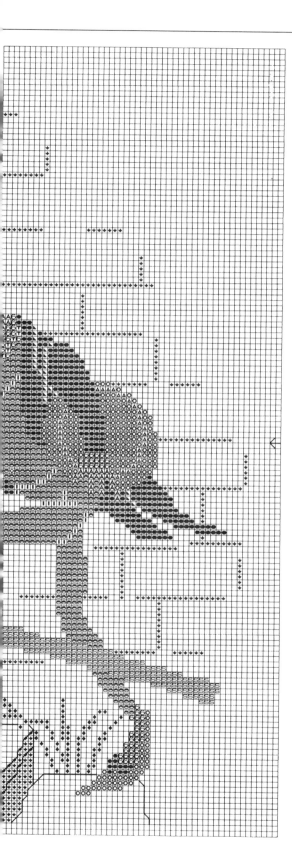

TEA-TIME TRAY

YOU WILL NEED

For a tray measuring 24cm (9½in) square:

*30cm (12in) square of cream evenweave
Hardanger, 18 threads to 2.5cm (1in)
DMC stranded embroidery cotton in the colours
given in the panel
No26 tapestry needle
Masking tape or strong thread for securing the
mounted fabric
Square wooden tray (for suppliers, see page 128)*

•

THE EMBROIDERY

With the prepared fabric stretched in an embroidery frame, see page 121, begin the cross stitching, using two strands of thread in the needle. Embroider the main characters first and then the background.

Finish by adding the backstitch details, using a single strand of thread.

Remove the design from the frame and steam press on the wrong side, if necessary.

ASSEMBLING THE TRAY

Using a soft pencil, mark the supplied mounting card both ways along the centre. This will help you to position the card exactly in the middle of the embroidery. Place the embroidery face down with the card on top and with the pencil lines and basting stitches matching.

Working on one side and then the opposite side, fold over the edges of the fabric on all sides, and secure with one or two pieces of masking tape. When you are sure the design is centred (if not, simply release the masking tape and adjust the fabric until it is correctly positioned), secure the corners firmly.

Turn in each corner to form a mitre (see page 123), and secure with masking tape. Next, finish securing the sides, stretching the fabric evenly, and finally, overcast the mitred corners to finish. Insert the mounted embroidery into the tray, following the manufacturer's instructions.

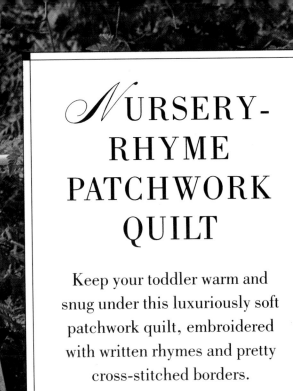

NURSERY-RHYME PATCHWORK QUILT

Keep your toddler warm and snug under this luxuriously soft patchwork quilt, embroidered with written rhymes and pretty cross-stitched borders.

Lucy Locket
Jack Be Nimble
Pease Pudding
Little Maid
Ride a Cock-horse
Ring-a-Ring-a-Roses
Little Tommy Tittlemouse
Jack Sprat
Hot Cross Buns
You Shall Have an Apple
Friday Night's Dream
Pippin Hill

NURSERY-RHYME PATCHWORK QUILT

YOU WILL NEED

For a quilt measuring 124.5cm × 95.5cm
(49½in × 38in):

*80cm (31in) of cream evenweave (Aida) fabric,
110cm (43in) wide, 14 threads to 2.5cm (1in) or
12 × 25.5cm (10in) squares of the same fabric
2m (2¼yds) of green polyester-cotton,
122cm (48in) wide
130cm (1½yds) of medium-weight synthetic
batting, 120cm (48in wide)
DMC stranded embroidery cotton in the colours
given in the panels on pages 42-53 inclusive
No24 tapestry needle
Matching sewing threads*

•

THE EMBROIDERY

Divide the evenweave fabric into twelve 25.5cm (10in) squares, marking the divisions with a pencil. This includes 12mm (½in) seam allowance on all sides. Using basting stitches, mark the centre both ways on each square, and following the instructions on page 121, stretch the fabric in a frame.

Begin the embroidery with the verses. These are worked in backstitch, using a single strand of thread in the needle (see page 125). Work the back-stitch over each square of the fabric to give a good shape to the letters. Complete the borders, using two strands of thread in the needle.

Remove the basting stitches and steam press on the wrong side, if needed. Cut out the 12 squares.

MAKING THE QUILT TOP

Following the cutting layout, cut the contrast fabric to the sizes given.

Begin by piecing together the quilt top, taking 12mm (½in) seam allowances throughout. The simplest way to do this is to make up the centre first and add the border last of all. Following the position guide, lay out the embroidered squares in number sequence.

Next, place the shorter contrast strips – H-I, J-K, L-M, N-O – between them to form four separate rows across. Baste and machine stitch individual rows.

In the same way, join the horizontal rows together by placing the longer strips (E, F, G) between, as shown in the diagram. Finally, add the side pieces (C and D) and then top and bottom pieces (A and B), to complete the quilt top. As you work, press the seams open.

COMPLETING THE QUILT

Trim the batting to measure 128.5cm × 99cm (50½in × 39in). Lay the top face down on a clean flat surface. Carefully lay the batting over the patchwork top, smoothing it out and matching edges. Lay the backing fabric over the batting, again matching edges. Pin and then baste the three layers together. Start with lines radiating from the centre. To avoid making a cluster of knots at the middle of the quilt, leave a long tail of thread at the centre and work to one edge before rethreading the needle and basting to the opposite edge. Also baste the layers together across and down the quilt.

Using matching sewing thread, or quilting thread, if your prefer, quilt around each square, along the seamlines.

You may find it easier to use a quilting hoop, leaving both hands free for stitching. It is helpful to wear a thimble on the second finger of your sew-ing hand, using it to guide the needle through the layers. Your lower hand, also with a thimble on the first or second finger, is used to check that the needle has passed through to the back and to push it back up to the surface. Try to make even stitches of the same length on both sides of the work.

When you have finished quilting, trim the batting back by 12mm (½in) all around the edge. Turn in the edges of the top and backing, folding the top fabric over the batting, and slipstitch. Alterna-tively, finish the quilt by trimming the batting, folding in and basting the top and backing seam allowances, and machine stitching, close to the edge.

POSITIONING GUIDE

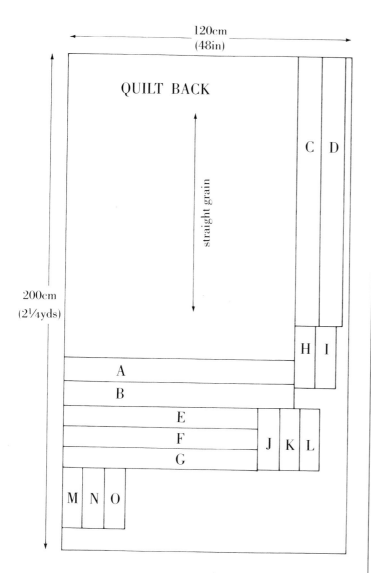

Cut quilt back 128.5cm × 98cm (50½in × 39in)

Cut two pieces (A, B) 99cm × 10cm (39in × 4in)

Cut two pieces (C, D) 113cm × 10cm (44½in × 4in)

Cut three pieces (E, F, G) 84cm × 9cm (33in × 3½in)

Cut eight pieces (H, I, J, K, L, M, N, O) 25.5cm × 9cm (10in × 3½in)

1 Lucy Locket	**7**	Little Tommy Tittlemouse
2 Jack be nimble	**8**	Jack Sprat
3 Pease pudding	**9**	Hot cross buns
4 Little maid	**10**	You shall have an apple
5 Ride a cock-horse	**11**	Friday night's dream
6 Ring-a-ring-a-roses	**12**	Pippin Hill

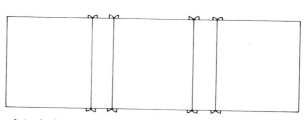

Join the horizontal rows together

LUCY LOCKET ▲

△ 973 yellow
● 605 pink
✱ 601 deep pink
  791 blue (bks lettering)
⊡ 910 green

JACK BE NIMBLE ▲

⊡ 973 yellow
● 554 lilac
  321 red (bks lettering)
✳ 910 green

PEASE PUDDING ▲

△ 973 yellow
● 605 pink
✱ 554 lilac (bks 550)
⊡ 550 mauve
   791 blue (bks lettering)
   910 green (bks top border)

LITTLE MAID ▲

⊡ 973 yellow
   321 red (bks lettering)
● 794 blue
✖ 910 green

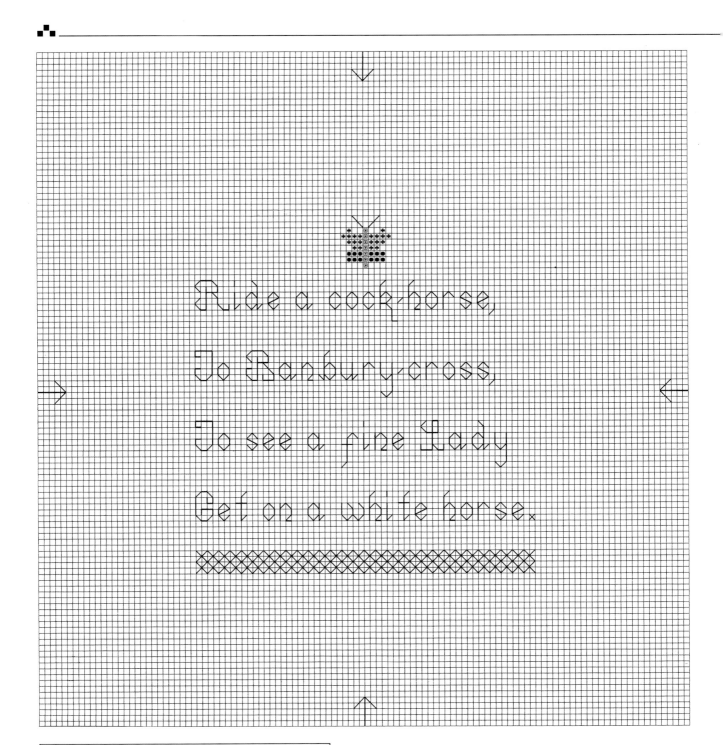

RIDE A COCK-HORSE ▲

✱ 605 pink
● 601 deep pink (bks trellis motif and antennae)
⊡ 794 pale blue
  791 blue (bks lettering)

RING-A-RING-A-ROSES ▲

⊡ 973 yellow
● 605 pink
  321 red (bks lettering)
✱ 910 green

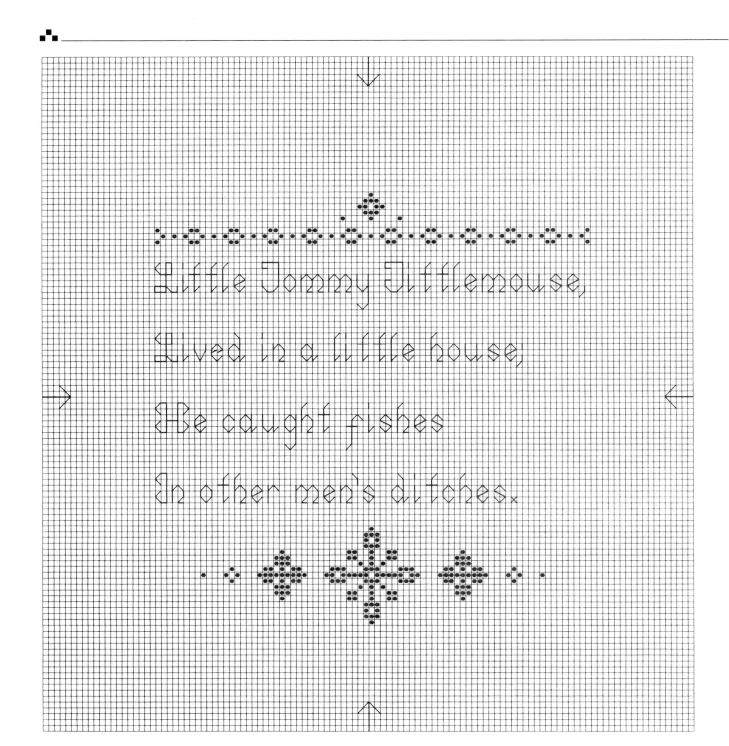

TOMMY TITTLEMOUSE ▲

● 794 pale blue
791 blue (bks lettering)

JACK SPRAT ▲

✱ 973 yellow
321 red (bks lettering)
● 910 green (bks flowers and trellis)

HOT CROSS BUNS ▲

- ⊡ 973 yellow
- ● 605 pink
  791 blue (bks lettering)
- ✚ 910 green

You shall have an apple,

You shall have a plum,

You shall have a rattle

When your daddy comes home.

YOU SHALL HAVE AN APPLE ▲

⊡ 973 yellow
● 321 red (bks lettering)
✱ 910 green

FRIDAY NIGHT'S DREAM ▲

⊡ 973 yellow

● 321 red

✱ 910 green
  791 blue (bks lettering)

PIPPIN HILL ▲

△ 973 yellow
● 321 red (bks lettering)
✳ 913 pale green
⊡ 910 dark green

*A*FTERNOON-TEA CLOTH

Delight your friends with this
perfect party piece – a tablecloth
embroidered with a deep border
of amusing animal motifs,
finished with mitred corners
and hemstitched in the
traditional way.

◆

THE CAT AND THE FIDDLE

Hey, diddle, diddle!
The cat and the fiddle,
The cow jumped over the moon,
The little dog laughed to see such fun,
And the dish ran away with the spoon.

AFTERNOON-
TEA CLOTH

YOU WILL NEED

For a tablecloth measuring 102cm (37in) square:

*110cm (43in) of cream evenweave (Aida) fabric,
110cm (43in) wide, 14 threads to 2.5cm (1in); an
8cm (3in) hem allowance is included on all sides
DMC stranded embroidery cotton in the colours
given in the panels; 3 skeins of pale yellow 834
for the hemstitching
No24 tapestry needle
Contrast basting thread*

PREPARING THE FABRIC

Begin by removing the selvedges from the fabric; check that it is perfectly square and press to remove any creases. Following the positioning diagram on page 58, mark the hem line with basting stitches, measuring 8cm (3in) in on all sides. Mark a second line in the same way, measuring a further 4cm (1½in) in: this is the base line for positioning the motifs. To mark the upright positioning lines, baste a line 11.5cm (4½in) at each side of the centre, on each side. Fold the fabric diagonally both ways; lightly finger press, and baste, as shown in the diagram.

THE EMBROIDERY

Using an embroidery hoop (see page 121) and following the colour charts given on the previous

DISH ▶

◆	white (bks 800)
○	951 flesh (and bks 3022)*
△	800 light blue
⊡	799 blue
●	820 royal blue
✱	823 dark blue

pages, complete the embroidery. Use two strands of thread in the needle throughout, with the exception of the eyebrows on the spoon; in this case, use a single strand. Finally, work the backstitching on top.

Following the instructions given on page 123, mitre the corners, and hemstitch the hem, using three strands of pale yellow 834 in the needle. Remove all the basting stitches and steam press the cloth on the wrong side.

THE CAT AND
THE FIDDLE ▶

÷   white (bks on paws
    310)
◺ 3047 pale yellow
I   435 ginger (bks 310)
⊡ 817 red
△ 814 dark red
↑   800 pale blue eyes
=   742 yellow (bks
    eyes 414)
◆ 801 brown
↓   938 dark brown
    (bks strings)
◣ 414 grey
✤ 310 black

Each of these little vignettes from the tablecloth could be used individually to decorate a tea tray, for example, or perhaps a child's pillowcase. Alternatively, you could make them into pages for a little cloth book.

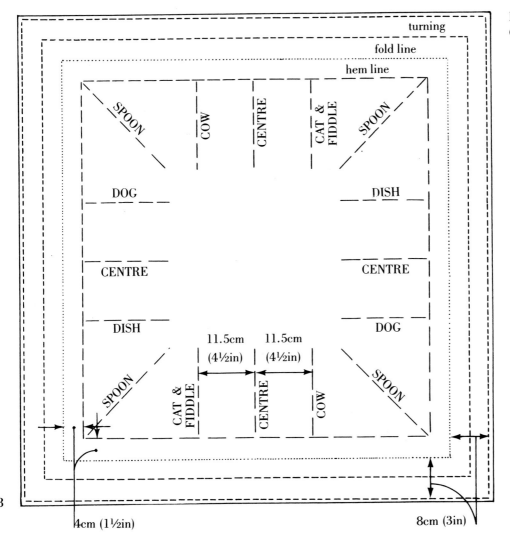

POSITIONING
GUIDE

turning

fold line

hem line

SPOON

COW

CENTRE

CAT &
FIDDLE

SPOON

DOG

DISH

CENTRE

CENTRE

DISH

DOG

11.5cm
(4½in)

11.5cm
(4½in)

SPOON

CAT &
FIDDLE

CENTRE

COW

SPOON

4cm (1½in)

8cm (3in)

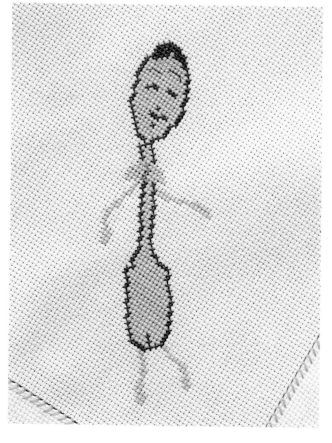

COW ►

○ white (bks cow's back
  435, flank 951)
↓ 3078 yellow
⊡ 951 apricot
✳ 3033 beige (bks horns
  612, hoofs 801)
● 435 brown
  (and bks 801*)
*Note: one additional
backstitch colour**

DOG ◄

÷ white
↑ 3033 flesh
S 352 pink
⊡ 817 red
△ 814 dark red
◣ 833 ochre
◆ 434 light brown
● 801 dark brown
↓ 3011 dark olive brown
◺ 415 light grey
○ 414 dark grey
✳ 310 black (bks 414)

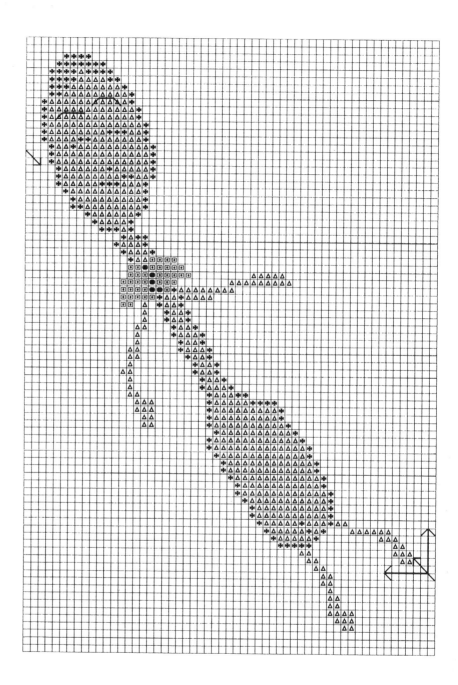

SPOON ▶

⊡ 800 light blue
● 799 blue
△ 762 light grey (bks 414)
✱ 414 dark grey

BIRTHDAY GREETINGS CARDS

These pleasing little birthday cards will delight any child recipient – and with a little help, children can stitch their own very special greetings.

THIS LITTLE PIG

This little pig went to market;
This little pig stayed at home;
This little pig had roast beef;
This little pig had none;

•

A LITTLE MAN

There was a little man, and he
had a little gun,
And his bullets were made of lead, lead, lead.

•

MISS MUFFET

Little Miss Muffet,
Sat on a tuffet,
Eating her curds and whey;
There came a big spider,
And sat down beside her,
And frightened Miss Muffet away.

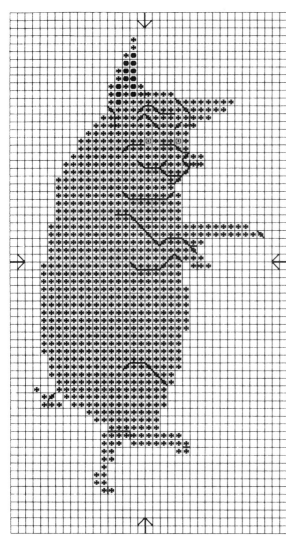

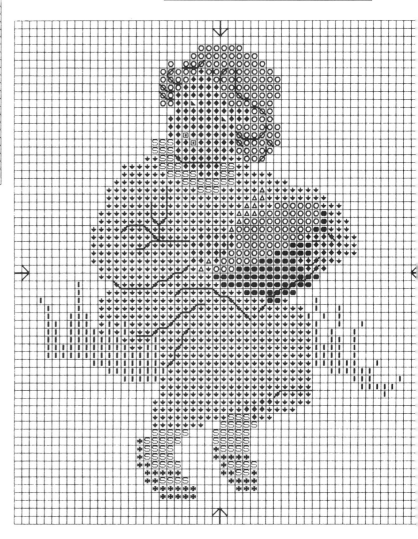

MISS MUFFET ▼

∽ 744 yellow
◆ 948 flesh (bks 352)
⊡ 352 pink
✻ 210 mauve
↓ 3325 pale blue (and bks 322*)
◣ 800 blue
I 3348 green
○ 739 beige (and bks 436*)
● 437 light brown (and bks 435*)
△ 415 pale grey
Note: 3 additional
*backstitch colours**

LITTLE PIG ▲

✻ 948 flesh (bks 352)
● 352 pink
⊡ 800 blue

64

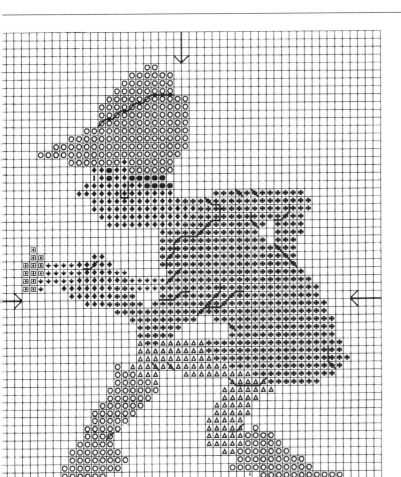

BIRTHDAY GREETINGS CARDS

YOU WILL NEED

For one birthday card, measuring 14cm × 9cm (5½in × 3½in) with a 9cm × 7cm (3½ × 2¾in) oval cut out:

17cm × 13cm (6¾in × 5in) of white Hardanger fabric, 22 threads to 2.5cm (1in)
DMC stranded embroidery cotton in the colours given in the appropriate panel
No 26 tapestry needle
Birthday card mount (for suppliers, see page 128)

•

THE EMBROIDERY

All three cards are stitched in the same way and on the same type of fabric.

Note that it is particularly important with embroidered cards to avoid excessive overstitching on the back, as this would cause unsightly lumps to show through on the right side.

Prepare the fabric and mount it in a small hoop, following the instructions on page 121. Referring to the chart, complete the cross stitching, using a single strand in the needle throughout. Embroider the main areas first and then finish with the backstitching. If necessary, steam press on the wrong side.

It is a good idea to leave the basting stitches in at this stage, as they will prove useful in helping to centre your design in the cut out window.

MAKING UP THE CARDS

With self-adhesive mounts, this could not be easier! Simply open out the three sections of the card. Trim the embroidery to about 12mm (½in) larger than the marked area around the cut-out window, and then, making sure that the motif is placed in the middle – measure an equal distance at each side of the basting – press it in place. Fold over and press the left-hand section, to cover the design and to give a neat permanent seal.

A LITTLE MAN ▲

- ◆ 948 flesh (and bks 352*)
- ✚ 3042 lilac
      (and bks 327*)
- I 800 blue
- △ 437 light brown
      (and bks 435*)
- ● 611 brown
- ↓ 415 pale grey
- ○ 453 grey (and bks 451*)
- ☐ 414 dark grey
  *Note: 4 additional backstitch colours**

MINIATURE PICTURES

What better way to build up a pretty collection of pictures, than to embroider them yourself?

• ■ •
■ ■

LITTLE MAID

'Little maid, pretty maid, Whither
goest thou?'
'Down in the forest to milk my cow.'
'Shall I go with thee?' 'No, not now;
When I send for thee, then come thou.'

•

ROCK-A-BYE, BABY,
ON THE TREE TOP

Rock-a-bye, baby, on the tree top!
When the wind blows the cradle will rock,
When the bough breaks the cradle will fall.
Down will come baby, bough, cradle and all.

•

QUITE WELL, QUITE HEARTY

A little girl quite well and hearty,
Thought she'd like to give a party.
But as her friends were quite shy and wary,
Nobody came but her own canary.

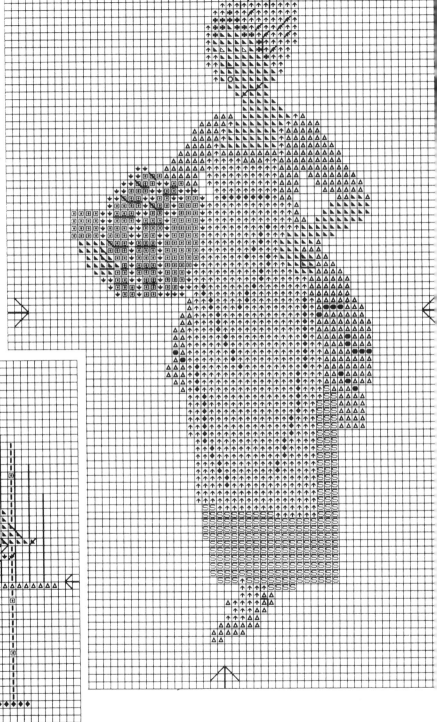

QUITE WELL, QUITE HEARTY ▼

- ○ 963 pink (bks 335, initial M 3041)
- ▣ 335 deep pink (bks 3041)
- ✦ 948 flesh
- ✲ 3041 purple (bks 3011)
- ❘ 966 green
- ◆ 3052 sap green
- ◣ 307 yellow (eye 833)
- △ 833 ochre (bks cage, bird's legs)
- ● 3011 dark brown

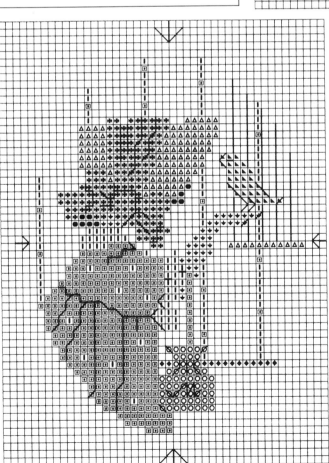

LITTLE MAID ◀

↑ white (and bks 318*)

◣ 948 flesh (bks 352)

○ 352 pink

◺ 800 blue

● 823 navy blue

△ 312 dark blue

⊡ 436 light brown (bks 434)

✳ 434 brown

◆ 415 pale grey

↓ 648 grey

Note: one additional backstitch colour*

ROCK-A-BYE BABY ▼

= white

↑ 726 yellow

I 676 gold

◣ 754 flesh
(bks eye 3688)

△ 3688 pink

● 602 deep pink

◺ 3756 pale blue
green (bks 519)

⊡ 519 blue green

S 955 pale green

↓ 913 green (bks twigs)

◆ 951 fawn

♣ 3011 brown

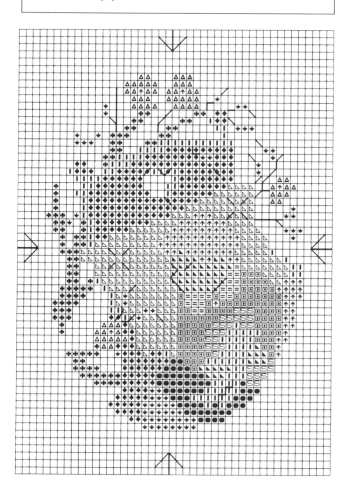

MINIATURE PICTURES

YOU WILL NEED

For the *Little Maid* picture, measuring
18cm × 13cm (7¼in × 5in):

*23cm × 18cm (9in × 7¼in) of blue evenweave
(Aida) fabric, 18 threads to 2.5cm (1in)
DMC stranded embroidery cotton in the colours
given in the appropriate panels
No 26 tapestry needle
Oval brass frame (for suppliers, see page 128)*

For *Quite Well*, *Quite Hearty*, and
Rock-a-Bye Baby miniatures, each measuring
11.5cm × 9cm (4½in × 3½in):

*28cm × 18cm (11in × 7¼in) of white evenweave
linen, 26 threads to 2.5 cm (1in)
DMC stranded embroidery cotton in the colours
given in the appropriate panels
No 26 tapestry needle
Two oval brass frames (for suppliers, see page 128)*

•

THE EMBROIDERY

Each picture is worked in the following way. With
the prepared fabric stretched in a hoop and the
centre marked both ways, see page 121, you are
ready to begin the cross stitching. Use two strands
of thread in the needle throughout, except for the
backstitching of *Little Maid*, which is worked in a
single strand. When working a fairly openweave
fabric, such as the linen used here, bear in mind
that threads should not be stranded across an open
area or they will be seen from the right side.

Remove the fabric from the frame and steam
press on the wrong side, if necessary.

MAKING UP THE PICTURES

Following the manufacturer's instructions for
assembling the pictures, remembering to check that
you have allowed sufficient fabric to fill the frame
before cutting out (see instructions for assembling
the Dressing-Table Set on page 108).

ℐRETTY PINCUSHIONS

Essential for needleworkers!
These pincushions are quick to
make, and roomy enough for a
good supply of pins.

TWO BIRDS

There were two birds sat on a stone,
Fa, la, la la, lal, de;
One flew away, then there was one,
Fa la, la, la lal, de;

LITTLE MAIDEN

Little maiden, better tarry;
Time enough next year to marry.
Hearts may change, And so may fancy;
Wait a little longer Nancy.

WEE WILLIE WINKIE

Wee Willie Winkie runs through the town;
Upstairs and downstairs, in his nightgown;
Rapping at the window, crying through
the lock,
'Are the children in their beds?
Now it's eight o'clock.'

PRETTY PINCUSHIONS

YOU WILL NEED

For the *Two Birds* pincushion, measuring
11.5cm (4½in) across:

*18cm (7¼in) square of cream evenweave
Hardanger, 16 threads to 2.5cm (1in)
DMC stranded embroidery cotton in the colours
given in the appropriate panel
No24 tapestry needle
Pincushion mould with wooden surround
(for suppliers, see page 128)*

For the *Little Maiden* pincushion, measuring
13cm (5in) square:

*Two 15cm (6in) squares of cream evenweave
(Aida) fabric, 14 threads to 2.5cm (1in)
110cm (1⅓yds) of pale pink parcel ribbon
DMC stranded embroidery cotton in the colours
given in the appropriate panel
No24 tapestry needle
Sufficient kapok or sheep's wool for filling
Matching sewing thread*

For *Wee Willie Winkie* pincushion, measuring
13cm (5in) square:

*Two 15cm (6in) squares of grey evenweave
(Aida 705) fabric, 18 threads to 2.5cm (1in)
60cm (24in) of narrow, deep turquoise cord
DMC stranded embroidery cotton in the colours
given in the appropriate panel
No26 tapestry needle
Sufficient kapok or sheep's wool for filling
Matching sewing threads*

•

THE EMBROIDERY

Work all three pincushions in the following way.
Prepare the fabric and stretch it in a hoop, see page
121, and taking one of the two squares only for the
Little Maiden and Wee Willie Winkie. Complete
the embroidery, using two strands of thread in the
needle. Remove from the frame and steam press on
the wrong side.

MAKING UP THE PINCUSHIONS

For the *Two Birds* cushion, lay the fabric face down,
with the wooden base centred on top, and draw
around with a soft pencil. Add at least a further
12mm (½in) outside the line and cut out. Run a
gathering thread along the pencil line; centre the
embroidery over the mould, and pin to hold. Pull
up the gathering thread; even out the gathers
around the underside of the mould, and secure the
thread firmly. Attach the mould to the base with the
screw provided.

For the *Little Maiden* and *Wee Willie Winkie*
cushions, in each case place the two sections right
sides together, and then pin and machine stitch
around the edge, taking 12mm (½in) seams and
leaving an 8cm (3in) opening in one side. Turn right
side out and insert the filling. Slipstitch the opening
to close.

For the *Little Maiden*, cut the ribbon into four
equal lengths and tie a bow around each corner,
taking the ribbon twice around before tying. For
Wee Willie Winkie, slipstitch the cord around the
edge (see page 124), looping the cord into a circle
approximately 12mm (½in) in diameter at each
corner, as shown in the photograph.

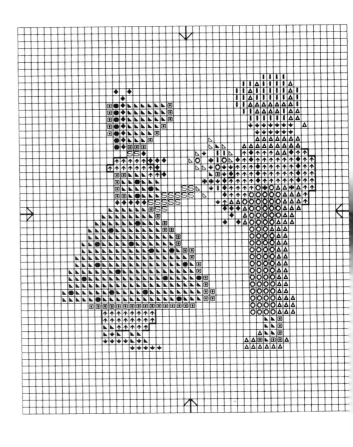

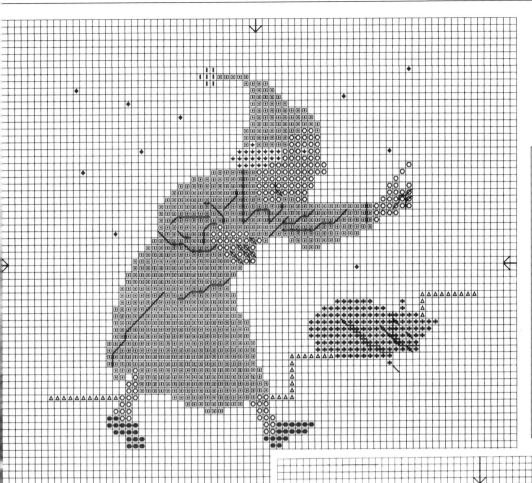

TWO BIRDS ▼

◺ white

◣ 444 yellow

△ 3733 pale pink

⊡ 893 deep pink

○ 3761 pale pink

✳ 334 blue (bks bird's
feet, small bird's
head and body)

● 322 dark blue
(bks eye, small
bird's wings)

⌇ 471 green (bks
tree and ground)

↓ 912 veridian green

Ι 3756 pale grey

WEE WILLIE WINKIE ▲

◆ 444 yellow

↓ 680 ochre

○ 948 flesh
(and bks 224*)

● 899 pink

⊡ 3761 pale blue
(bks 807)

Ι 807 blue

△ 644 stone

✳ 413 dark grey
(and bks 318*)

*Note: 2 additional backstitch colours**

LITTLE MAIDEN ◄

↑ white (bks
bloomers and
collar 471, bks
boy's shirt 799)

Ι 834 straw

⌇ 948 flesh

◣ 605 pale pink

⊡ 3731 pink

● 602 deep pink

✳ 892 red

○ 3766 light blue

△ 799 blue

◺ 3348 bright green

◆ 471 green

↓ 3011 brown

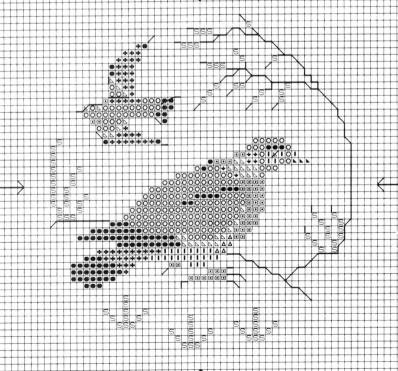

COFFEE TIME COMPANIONS

Pretty and practical! Keep your coffee piping hot and your table top protected with this snugly-fitting cosy and coffee-pot stand, and so that you don't miss your coffee break, keep the carriage clock to hand.

POLLY PUT THE KETTLE ON

Polly, put the kettle on,
Polly, put the kettle on,
Polly, put the kettle on,
We'll all have tea.

•

COFFEE AND TEA

Molly, my sister and I fell out,
And what do you think it was all about?
She loved coffee and I loved tea,
And that was the reason we couldn't agree.

•

HICKORY, DICKORY, DOCK

Hickory, dickory, dock!
The mouse ran up the clock;
The clock struck one,
And down he ran,
Hickory, dickory, dock.

COFFEE-POT COSY

YOU WILL NEED

To fit a single-sized coffee pot, 15cm (6in) high:

46cm × 25cm (18in × 10in) of cream evenweave fabric (Aida), 14 threads to 2.5cm (1in)
46cm × 25cm (18in × 10in) of pink lawn lining fabric
46cm × 25cm (18in × 10in) of lightweight synthetic batting
110cm (1⅓yd) of pink bias binding, 2.5cm (1in) wide
DMC stranded embroidery cotton in the colours given in the panel
No24 tapestry needle
Matching sewing thread

●

THE EMBROIDERY

Cut the evenweave fabric in half to give two pieces, each measuring 23cm × 25cm (9in × 10in). With one section prepared and stretched in a hoop, see page 121, baste the positioning lines for the motif as on the chart given opposite.

Using two strands of thread in the needle throughout, complete the embroidery, working the cross stitching first and then the backstitching. If necessary, steam press the finished embroidery on the wrong side.

MAKING UP THE COSY

Make the paper pattern for the cosy by enlarging the diagram (given opposite) on plain notepaper, see page 122 and cut out. These measurements include 12mm (½in) seam allowances all round.

Place the pattern on the straight grain of the fabric and cut out the evenweave, lining fabric and batting as instructed.

For the loop, cut 13cm (5in) of bias binding. Fold in the edges, slipstitch and fold the length in half to form a loop. With the raw edges pointing towards the edge of the fabric, baste the loop inside the seam line at the centre of the front section of the cosy.

Take the remaining bias binding; fold it lengthwise in half, and gather along the unfolded long edge. With the gathered edge just inside the seam allowance, lay the frill on the right side of the front section, along the curved edge, easing the gathers to fit. Pin and baste.

Baste batting to the wrong side of each top section and then trim the batting back to clear the seam allowance. Using either catchstitch or herringbone stitch, secure the batting to the seam allowance. With right sides inside, baste and machine stitch the two sections together, 12mm (½in) from the outer edge. Trim the seamline to measure 6mm (¼in). Make a single turning around the lower edge folding it over the batting, and baste. Carefully snip into the curved seam, and turn the cosy right side out.

With right sides together, join the lining sections. Make a single turning around the lower edge and baste. Slip the lining inside the cosy and catchstitch to the batting at the centre top.

Baste and then slipstitch the lining to the cosy at the lower edge. Remove all basting stitches to complete the cosy.

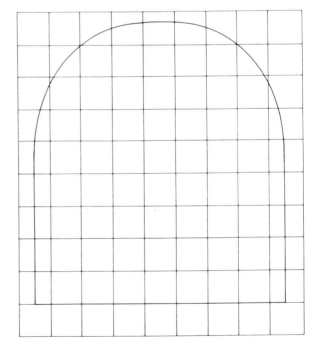

Each square = 2.5cm (1in)
Cut two from evenweave
Cut two from lining
Cut two from batting
12mm (½in) seam allowances included

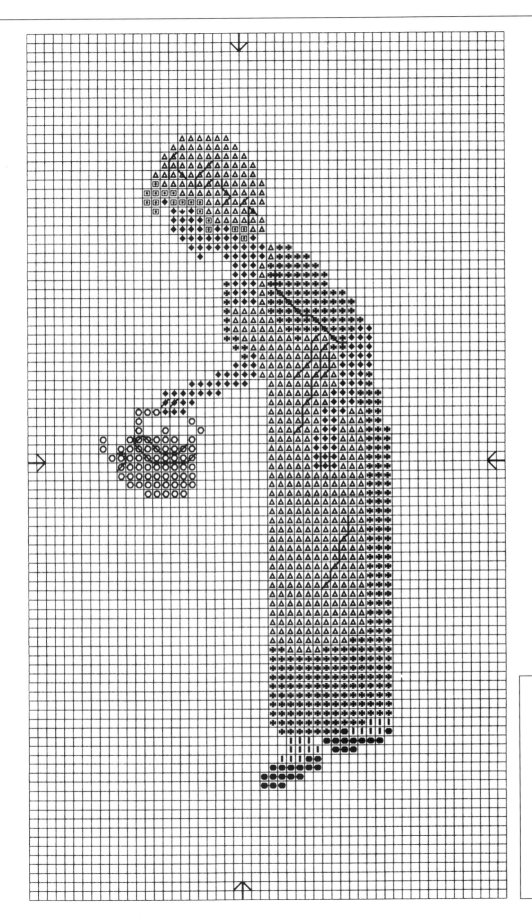

POLLY, PUT THE
KETTLE ON ◄

I white

○ 834 gold (bks 832)

⊡ 832 ochre

◆ 948 flesh (bks 453)

✱ 335 deep pink
    (bks 3041)

● 3041 purple

↓ 793 blue

△ 453 grey (bks 3041)

COFFEE AND TEA ▲

I white (bks 927)

◣ 834 gold (bks 642)

○ 3774 flesh (bks 224)

● 224 dusky pink

◆ 3756 pale blue

△ 927 blue green

⊡ 926 deep blue green

↓ 642 coffee (bks 371)

✤ 371 brown (bks kettle handle)

COFFEE-POT STAND

YOU WILL NEED

An overall hexagonal measuring 18cm (7in) with a 13cm (5in) circular centre:

*20cm (8in) square of cream Hardanger fabric,
18 threads to 2.5cm (1in)
DMC stranded embroidery cotton in the colours
given in the panel
No26 tapestry needle
coffee pot stand (for suppliers, see page 128)*

THE EMBROIDERY

Working in a hoop with the centre lines basted both ways, see page 121, begin the embroidery. Following the chart given opposite, use two strands of thread in the needle for the cross stitching and a single strand for the backstitching. Leaving the basting stitches in place, steam press the finished embroidery on the wrong side.

ASSEMBLING THE STAND

To get an exact fit, cut out the embroidery, following the instructions given for The Traditional Dressing-Table Set on page 108. After that, assemble the stand according to the manufacturer's instructions.

CARRIAGE CLOCK

YOU WILL NEED

For clock measuring overall 16.5cm × 13cm
(6½in × 5in) with a 13cm × 9cm
(5in × 3½in) face:

*20cm × 16.5cm (8in × 6½in) of cream
Hardanger fabric, 16 threads to 2.5cm (1in)
DMC stranded embroidery cotton in the colours
given in the panel
No 24 tapestry needle
Carriage clock (for suppliers, see page 128)
Strong thread for mounting the embroidery*

Alternative suggestions for the clock face numerals.

THE EMBROIDERY

It should be possible to stitch such a small amount of embroidery in the hand without running the risk of distorting the fabric. Whichever way you choose to work, mark the centre both ways with basting stitches. Note that the centre of the clock face is higher than the centre of the embroidery, and should also be marked with a pencil.

Using two strands of thread in the needle throughout, follow the chart and complete the embroidery. When stitching the numerals, remember to start and finish with each one; do not strand from one to another or this will show on the right side. Steam press the finished embroidery on the wrong side.

ASSEMBLING THE CLOCK

Follow the manufacturer's instructions for mounting the embroidery and assembling the clock. See also Basic Skills, page 124, for lacing and mounting an embroidery.

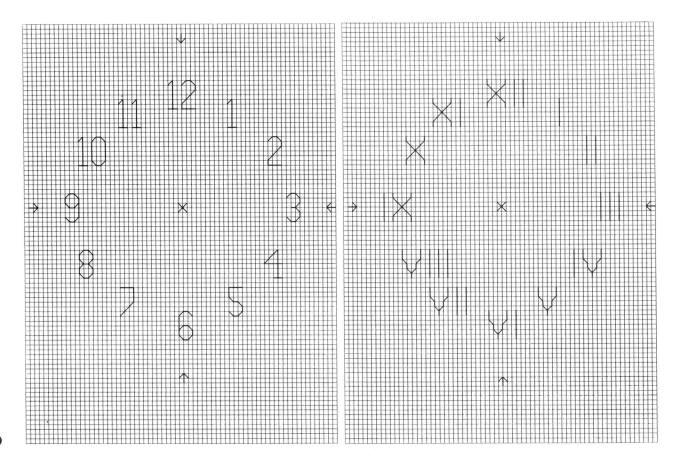

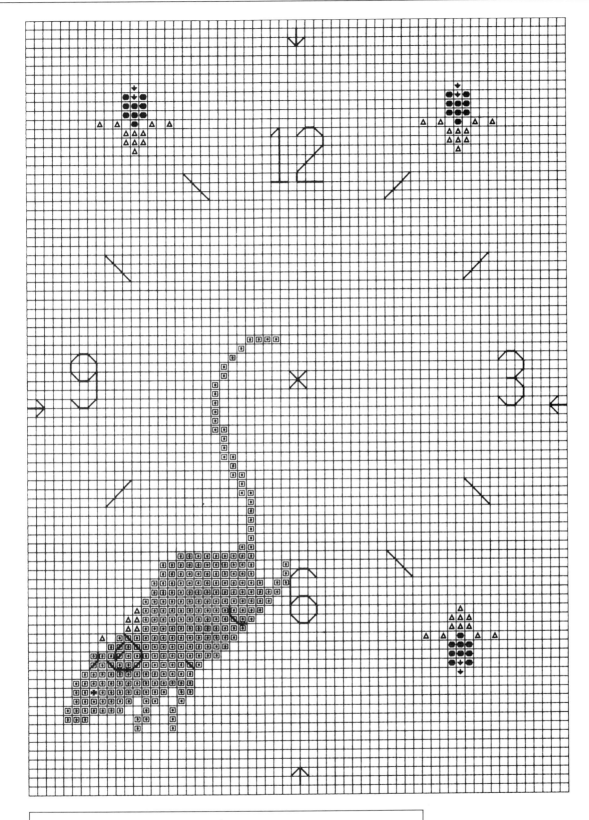

HICKORY, DICKORY, DOCK ▲

↓ 832 yellow   △ 472 green   ✳ 310 black

● 3731 pink   ⊡ 3023 fawn (bks 610)   (bks numerals)

CHRISTMAS GREETINGS CARDS

What better way to personalize your greetings than to embroider them yourself? Using prepared mounts, you can give them a truly professional finish.

LITTLE JACK HORNER

Little Jack Horner sat in a corner,
Eating a Christmas pie;
He put in his thumb, and pulled out a plum,
And said, 'What a good boy am I!'

DAME GET UP

Dame, get up and bake your pies,
Bake your pies, bake your pies,
Dame get up and bake your pies
On Christmas day in the morning.

I SAW THREE SHIPS

I saw three ships come sailing by,
Come sailing by, come sailing by,
I saw three ships come sailing by,
On New Year's day in the morning.

CHRISTMAS
GREETINGS CARDS

YOU WILL NEED

For the *Little Jack Horner* card, measuring overall 20cm × 14.5cm (8in × 5¾in), with rectangular portrait cut out, 14cm × 9.5cm (5½in × 3¾in):

*23cm × 18cm (9in × 7¼in) of blue evenweave fabric (Aida), 18 threads to 2.5cm (1in)
DMC stranded embroidery cotton in the colours given in the appropriate panel
No26 tapestry needle
Card mount (for suppliers, see page 128)*

For the *Dame Get Up* card, measuring overall 20cm × 14cm (8in × 5½in) with oval portrait cut out, 14cm × 9.5cm (5½in × 3¾in):

*23cm × 18cm (9in × 7¼in) of white evenweave cotton (Linda), 27 threads to 2.5cm (1in)
DMC stranded embroidery cotton in the colours given in the appropriate panel
No26 tapestry needle
Card mount (for suppliers, see page 128)*

For the *I Saw Three Ships* card, measuring overall 20cm × 14.5cm (8in × 5¾in) with rectangular landscape cut out, 14cm × 9.5cm (5½in × 3¾in):

*23cm × 18cm (9in × 7¼in) of white (natural) linen, 26 threads to 2.5cm (1in)
DMC stranded embroidery cotton in the colours given in the appropriate panel
No26 tapestry needle
Card mount (for suppliers, see page 128)*

•

THE EMBROIDERY

Prepare the fabric for each individual card in the same way and stretch it in a frame, see page 121.

Bear in mind that very openweave linens tend to fray, so it is a good idea to overcast the edges beforehand.

Complete the cross stitching, using two strands of thread in the needle throughout. Finish by adding the backstitch details, using a single strand of thread. Remove the embroidery from the frame; take out the basting stitches, and steam press on the wrong side.

ASSEMBLING THE CARDS

Open out the self-adhesive card mount; centre your embroidered design over the window; trim to size, and fold over the left-hand side section. Press to secure. See also Birthday Greetings Cards on page 64.

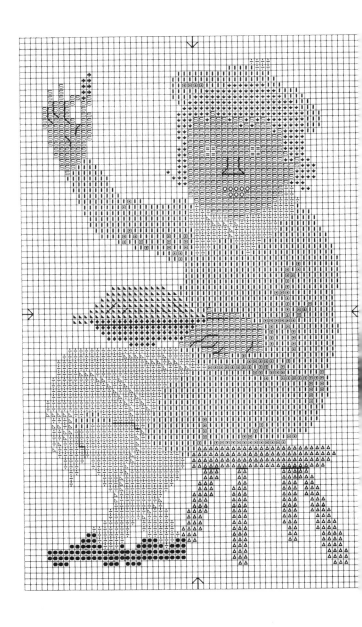

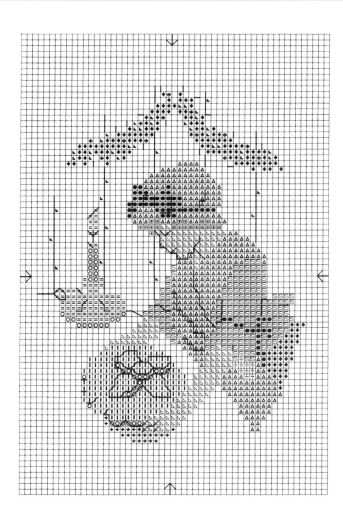

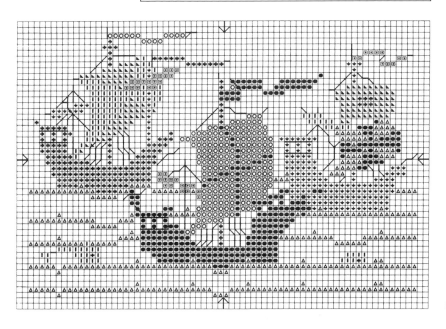

85

A CHILD'S PICTURE

Every picture tells a story – and this embroidery, stitched in minute detail, tells of a doting farmer and his luckless pony-ride in true pictorial style.

LITTLE DISASTER

Once there lived a little man,
Where a little river ran,
And he had a little farm and little dairy O!
And he had a little plough,
And a little dappled cow,
Which he often called his pretty little fairy O!

Then to make the story short,
Little pony with a snort,
Lifted up his heels so very clever O!
And the man he tumbled down,
And he nearly cracked his crown,
And this only made the matter worse than ever O!

LITTLE DISASTER ▶

T white
H 745 pale yellow
  (and bks 742*)
S 677 pale gold
  (and bks 729*)
÷ 722 orange
△ 783 ochre
⊝ 951 flesh
  (and bks 758*)
| 435 rust
  (and bks 300*)
◇ 519 blue
↑ 472 pale green
◺ 469 sap green
  (and bks 935*)
↓ 503 blue green
  (and bks 500*)
‖ 3345 dark green
✕ 712 cream
  (and bks 842*)
◣ 822 beige (bks 640)
✳ 3045 light brown
  (bks 435)
  839 dark brown
  (bks 435)
◆ 3072 pale grey
○ 926 blue grey
  (and bks 311*)
● 310 black (bks 712)
  *Note: 8 additional
  backstitch colours**

A CHILD'S PICTURE

YOU WILL NEED

For an unframed picture measuring
23cm (9in) square:

*35cm (14in) square of blue evenweave (Aida)
fabric, 18 threads to 2.5cm (1in)
23cm (9in) square of lightweight batting
DMC stranded embroidery cotton in the colours
given in the panel
No26 tapestry needle
23cm (9in) square of 3mm (⅛in) cardboard
Masking tape for securing the mounted fabric
Picture frame of your choice*

•

THE EMBROIDERY

Referring to the instructions on page 121, stretch
the prepared fabric in a frame. Using two strands
of thread in the needle and carefully following the
chart, begin the embroidery. Work the outline and
the two horizontal dividing lines first, making sure
you count the correct number of threads between.

Finish the cross stitching and, using a single
strand of thread, work the backstitching to complete the embroidery.

Remove the embroidery from the frame and, if
necessary, steam press on the wrong side.

FRAMING THE PICTURE

To offset the embroidery, the picture here includes
a border of background fabric 2cm (¾in) wide,
which you can easily adjust to suit your own prefer-
ence. You may wish, for example, to add a
decorative outer border in cross stitching, choosing
one of the borders given at the end of the book.
Also, to give the finished picture a slightly padded
look, a layer of lightweight batting is inserted
between the fabric and mounting card.

Mount the picture, following the instructions
given for the Tea-time Tray on page 36, before
finally inserting it into the picture frame.

BORDERED PICTURES

Transform a simple illustration into an appealing picture by framing it with a border of motifs taken from the design itself.

JACK AND JILL

Jack and Jill went up the hill
To fetch a pail of water;
Jack fell down and broke his crown
And Jill came tumbling after.

•

TOMMY TITTLEMOUSE

Little Tommy Tittlemouse
Lived in a little house;
He caught fishes
In other men's ditches.

•

TOM, TOM, THE PIPER'S SON

Tom, Tom, the piper's son,
Stole a pig and away he ran.
The pig was eat and Tom was beat,
And Tom went crying down the street.

BORDERED PICTURES

YOU WILL NEED

For the *Jack and Jill* picture, measuring
23cm × 16.5cm (9in × 6½in):

*30cm × 24cm (12in × 9½in) of cream evenweave
(Aida) fabric, 14 threads to 2.5 cm (1in)
DMC stranded embroidery cotton in the colours
given in the panel on page 93
No24 tapestry needle
24cm × 18cm (9½in × 7¼in) of 3mm (⅛in)
cardboard for mounting the embroidery
24cm × 18cm (9½in × 7¼in) of lightweight
synthetic batting
Masking tape or strong thread for securing the
mounted fabric
Picture frame of your choice*

For the *Tommy Tittlemouse* picture, measuring
16.5cm × 14cm (6½in × 5½in):

*23cm × 25cm (9in × 10in) of white evenweave
(Aida) fabric, 14 threads to 2.5 cm (1in)
DMC stranded embroidery cotton in the colours
given in the panel on this page
No24 tapestry needle
18cm × 15cm (7¼in × 6in) of 3mm (⅛in)
cardboard for mounting the embroidery
18cm × 15cm (7¼in × 6in) of lightweight
synthetic batting
Masking tape or strong thread and picture frame,
see above*

For *Tom, Tom, the Piper's Son* picture, measuring
20cm × 16.5cm (8in × 6½in):

*23cm × 24cm (9in × 9½in) of blue evenweave
(Aida) fabric, 14 threads to 2.5 cm (1in)
DMC stranded embroidery cotton in the colours
given in the panel on page 94
No24 tapestry needle
21.5cm × 18cm (8½in × 7¼in) of 3mm (⅛in)
cardboard for mounting the embroidery
21.5cm × 18cm (8½in × 7¼in) of lightweight
synthetic batting
Masking tape or strong thread and picture frame,
see above*

The embroidery for all three pictures is worked in
the same way.

Begin by preparing the edges of the fabric and
stretching it in an embroidery frame. Next, baste
the centre lines in both directions, following the
instructions given on page 121.

Working with two strands of thread in the
needle throughout, complete the cross stitching,
referring to the appropriate chart and colour key.
Finish embroidering the main characters before
working the background and, finally, stitching
the border.

Remove the fabric from the frame and, if necessary, steam press on the wrong side. Do not take
out the basting stitches at this stage – they will
be used as a guide when centring the mounting
card on the fabric.

JACK AND JILL ▲

- ⊟ white (bks 827)
- △ 729 yellow
- ÷ 3046 corn (bks 3072)
- ↑ 950 flesh (bks 224)
- △ 224 pink (bks 611)
- ● 3731 deep pink
- = 827 pale blue (bks 3052)
- ○ 799 blue
- ↓ 772 light green
- ◆ 3052 sage green (bks 829)
- ⊡ 611 brown (bks 829)
- ✱ 829 dark brown (bks bucket)
- ◣ 3072 grey (and bks 453*)
- I 472 green

Note: one additional backstitch colour*

TOMMY TITTLEMOUSE ◀

- ↑ white (bks 642)
- ⊟ 726 yellow (bks 732)
- ○ 741 orange
- ↓ 832 ochre
- △ 948 flesh (bks eye 732)
- ◆ 224 pink
- ⊡ 3328 red
- ÷ 598 blue
  (bks water, clouds)

- ✱ 732 olive (bks birds and fishing line; bks 832)
- = 3348 light green
- I 913 green
- ◣ 943 dark green
- S 642 fawn (bks 535)
- △ 640 brown
- ● 535 dark grey

MAKING UP THE PICTURES

To facilitate framing, an extra 12mm (½in) has been allowed each way, but the size of the cardboard can easily be adjusted to suit the measurements of a particular frame. You may prefer to add a much wider border of fabric around the embroidery before mounting and framing. In this case, remember to allow for the additional measurement to the ground fabric, and mounting board, before you begin the embroidery.

The pictures here have also been given a slightly padded look by inserting a layer of batting between the embroidery and the cardboard mount.

Make up the pictures in the same way as the Tea-time Tray on page 36, but before you attach the fabric to the back of the card, draw around the edges of the card with pencil. Remove the card, place the batting in position on the embroidery, and then replace the card on top and continue as before.

Finally, insert the finished picture into your frame. A simple alternative to traditional framing is to display your embroidery in a glass frame. Here, the fabric is placed between two pieces of glass, which are clipped around the edges.

TOM, TOM,
THE PIPER'S
SON ▶

I	white
S	948 flesh
	(bks 352)
✦	754 pale pink
△	352 pink
◣	977 orange
↑	834 ochre
⊡	436 brown
●	869 dark brown
○	800 blue
◆	503 green
△	502 mid-green
✱	500 dark green

FRINGED GUEST TOWEL

This delightful guest towel
takes very little time to make.
It has an amusing motif
embroidered in a relatively large
stitch, and the short edges are
simply hemstitched and fringed.

A CAT CAME FIDDLING

A cat came fiddling out of a barn,
With a pair of bagpipes under her arm;
She could sing nothing but fiddle-de-dee,
The mouse has married the bumblebee,
Pipe, cat; dance, mouse –
We'll have a wedding at our good house.

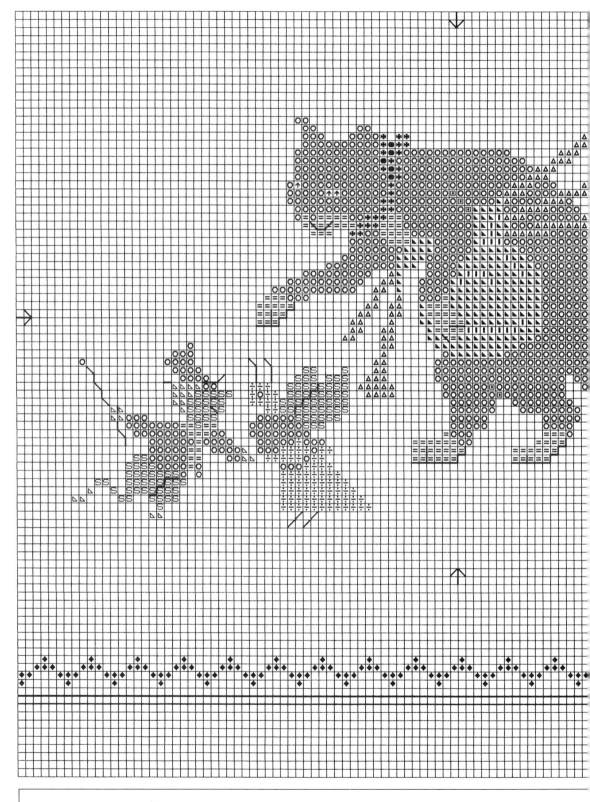

A CAT CAME FIDDLING ▲

= white (bks 927)	▮ 869 brown
÷ 725 yellow	△ 801 dark brown
◣ 729 ochre	◺ 778 pink
	✳ 304 red

◆ 3705 vermilian red
● 902 dark red
↑ 472 light green
↓ 3347 green

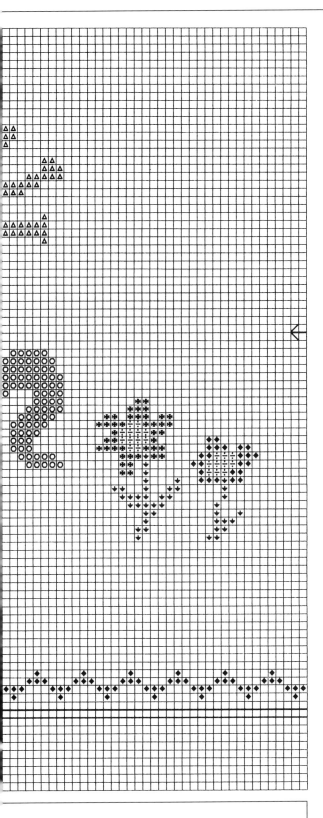

- ⊑ 927 pale grey (bks 413)
- ⊡ 413 dark grey
- ◯ 310 black (bks hat brim, walking stick, bee's antennae and feet)

FRINGED
GUEST TOWEL

YOU WILL NEED

For a guest towel measuring 69cm × 42cm
(27in × 16½in):

*69cm × 47cm (27in × 18½in) of cream or white
huckaback, 10 stitches to 2.5cm (1in); any suitable
soft fabric, such as Zweigart's Tula, can be used
DMC stranded embroidery cotton in the colours
given in the panel, plus one skein of ecru
for the hemstitching
No18 tapestry needle
Matching sewing thread*

•

THE EMBROIDERY

Hems Hemstitch the finished edges of the guest
towel before completing the cross stitch motif in a
hoop.

For the fringed edges, follow the instructions
given on page 125 and work a single row of hemstitching across the two short edges, placing the
stitching line 4cm (1½in) in from the raw edge; first
making sure the raw edge is cut straight along the
grain. Using three strands of matching stranded
cotton in the needle, work over two squares across
and one square deep for each stitch.

On the two long edges, first baste a 12mm (½in)
double turning. With the right side facing, hemstitch to hold the hem in place. Work the hemstitching as before, but make sure when passing the
needle behind that it enters the fabric at right
angles – not only to secure the hem but to give a
neat appearance to the stitches on the wrong side.

Motif Baste the positioning lines for the embroidered motif, following the chart given opposite, and
then, referring to the colour key, complete the cross
stitching.

If needed, steam press on the wrong side. Finish
by removing the threads below the hemstitching to
complete the fringed edges.

VICTORIAN-STYLE FOOTSTOOL

The enduring charm of heraldic design – adapted here on this traditional rosewood footstool – is sure to make it a family favourite.

THE LION AND THE UNICORN

The lion and the unicorn were fighting for
the crown,
The lion beat the unicorn all around the town.
Some gave them white bread, and some gave
them brown,
Some gave them plum-cake and sent them
out of town.

VICTORIAN-STYLE FOOTSTOOL

YOU WILL NEED

For a footstool measuring 30cm (12in) across:

*46cm (18in) square of grey evenweave (Aida 718)
fabric, 14 threads to 2.5cm (1in)
DMC stranded embroidery cotton in the colours
given in the panel
No24 tapestry needle
Round footstool with wooden surround
(for suppliers, see page 128)*

•

THE EMBROIDERY

Prepare the fabric and stretch it in an embroidery frame, following the instructions given on page 121.

The cross stitching is worked with two strands of thread in the needle, with the exception of the unicorn. This is worked in three strands to emphasize the colour. Begin the cross stitching, working outwards from the middle, leaving the white unicorn until last.

Remove the finished embroidery from the frame, and if necessary, steam press it on the wrong side.

MAKING UP THE FOOTSTOOL

Follow the manufacturer's instructions for assembling the footstool, but first make a preliminary check to see if, with the top fabric (the embroidery) included, the mould fits snugly inside the outer wooden frame. If not, then it is a good idea to add a layer of synthetic batting underneath the top fabric.

Complete the assembly, but before using the footstool, coat the embroidered surface with a proprietry dust-repellant spray, as recommended by upholsterers.

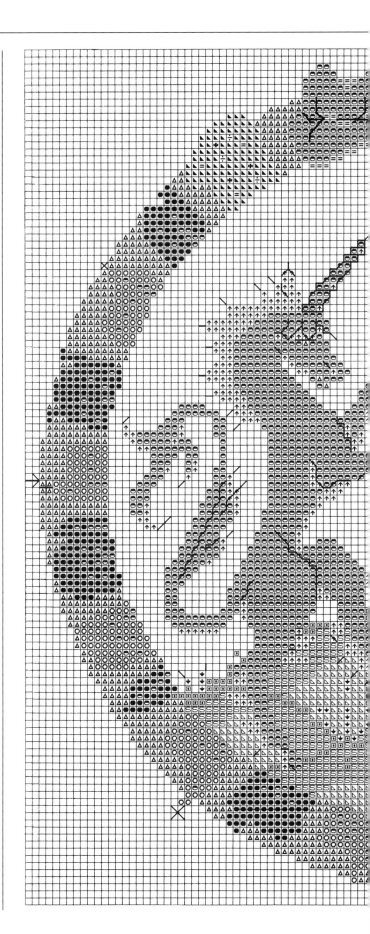

THE LION AND THE UNICORN ◀

- ⬬ white (bks 928)
- ◣ 822 cream
- ÷ 725 yellow (bks 831)
- = 676 corn (bks on white bread)
- ○ 734 gold (bks 831)
- ◆ 831 ochre
- ● 3712 red
- △ 598 blue
- ◿ 3348 light green
- ⌇ 989 green
- ⊡ 992 veridian green
- ✦ 320 dark green
- ✶ 3045 brown (bks on brown bread)
- ↑   bread)
-    928 grey

TIED-ON PILLOW COVER

Dress up a plain yellow pillow with this pretty tied-on cover, embroidered on crisp white cotton.

❖

LITTLE BOY BLUE

Little Boy Blue, come blow your horn!
The sheep's in the meadow, the cow's
in the corn.
Where's the boy that looks after the sheep?
He's under the haycock fast asleep.
Will you wake him? No, not I,
For if I do, he'll be sure to cry.

TIED-ON
PILLOW COVER

YOU WILL NEED

For a pillow cover measuring 46cm × 35cm
(18in × 14in):

*48.5cm × 38cm (19in × 15in) of white evenweave
(Aida) fabric, 14 threads to 2.5cm (1in)
48.5cm × 38cm (19in × 15in) of white backing
fabric, either fine cotton or linen
250cm (2⅔yds) of cornflower blue satin ribbon,
2cm (¾in) wide
140cm (1½yds) of cornflower blue bias binding
DMC stranded embroidery cotton in the colours
given in the panel
No24 tapestry needle
Matching sewing thread*

•

THE EMBROIDERY

With the prepared fabric stretched in a frame, see
page 121, baste the positioning lines for the motif
at the bottom left of the fabric, 12cm (4¾in) in from
both sides, following the chart opposite.

Using two strands of thread in the needle
throughout, work all the cross stitching first and
then the backstitching.

Take out the basting stitches; remove the fabric
from the frame, and steam press on the wrong side.

MAKING UP THE PILLOW COVER

With right sides together, baste the top
and backing fabric along the two long edges.
Machine stitch, taking 12mm (½in) seams. Press
the seams open.

For the ties, cut the ribbon into eight equal
lengths. With the wrong side facing, baste them
in pairs to each of the short edges, placing
them 10cm (4in) in from the corners (see the
diagram below).

Cover the short edges with bias binding, at the
same time enclosing the ribbon ends. Overlap the
raw edges of the binding at the seams. Press and
turn through to the right side. Slip the cover over
a contrast pillow and tie in place.

LITTLE BOY BLUE ▶

- ◺ white (bks 341)
- ⊑ 744 yellow (bks 738)
- ↓ 738 corn
- ◆ 834 deep yellow
- I 3779 flesh (bks 3712)
- △ 3712 red (bks 3052)
- ○ 341 blue (bks 792)
- ● 792 dark blue (bks eye;
  bks 3011)
- ✳ 3052 olive
- ⊡ 3011 brown

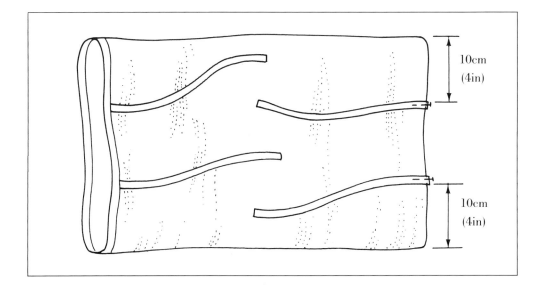

10cm
(4in)

10cm
(4in)

TRADITIONAL DRESSING-TABLE SET

Embroider these delightful
dressing-table accessories,
choosing – if you like – an
alternative background colour to
suit your bedroom decor.

CURLY-LOCKS

Curly-locks, Curly-locks, wilt thou be mine?
Thou shalt not wash the dishes, nor yet
feed the swine;
But sit upon a cushion, and sew a fine seam,
And feed upon strawberries, sugar and cream.

SLEEP BABY, SLEEP

Sleep, baby, sleep,
Our cottage vale is deep:
The little lamb is on the green,
With woolly fleece so soft and clean –
Sleep, baby, sleep.

TWINKLE, TWINKLE, LITTLE STAR

Twinkle, twinkle, little star,
How I wonder what you are!
Up above the sky so high,
Like a diamond in the sky.

TRADITIONAL DRESSING-TABLE SET

YOU WILL NEED

For the dressing-table set – handmirror with back measuring 13cm × 11.5cm (5in × 4½in), hairbrush with back measuring 10cm × 9cm (4in × 3½in), trinket box with lid measuring 10cm (4in) across:

45cm × 20cm (18in × 8in) of blue evenweave
fabric (Aida 503), 18 threads to 2.5cm (1in)
DMC stranded embroidery cotton in the colours
given in the panels
No26 tapestry needle
Dressing-table set, plus trinket box
(for suppliers, see page 128)

●

THE EMBROIDERY

As an alternative to setting individual pieces of fabric in a small embroidery hoop, you may find it easier and more economical to work all three designs on one piece of fabric, stretched in a rectangular frame. In either case, use basting stitches to divide the area into three equal sections measuring 20cm × 15cm (8in × 6in).

Baste the central positioning lines on each section, ready for cross stitching the motifs. Referring to the charts, complete the embroidery; use two strands of thread throughout, with the exception of the stars on the trinket box, which are worked in a single strand. To make the stars, see Eyelet Stitch on page 125. Remove the finished embroidery from the frame and, if necessary, steam press on the wrong side.

ASSEMBLING THE DRESSING-TABLE SET

The paper templates supplied by the manufacturers may vary in size so, in order to get an exact fit for each piece, cut out the embroidery, using the template supplied with each piece, but first mark the centre on the template both ways in pencil. In each case, place the template with the marked side on the wrong side of the embroidery; match the pencil

lines to the basting stitches, and draw around with a soft pencil. This will help you to centre your embroidery. Before cutting out, place the template inside the particular frame and check to see how much more fabric, if any, should be included beyond the pencil line. This is a critical stage in the assembly, because the return on the frames is very shallow and therefore does not allow for the fabric to be cut too small. Cut out the fabric and remove the basting stitches.

Complete the assembly of all three pieces, following the manufacturer's instructions.

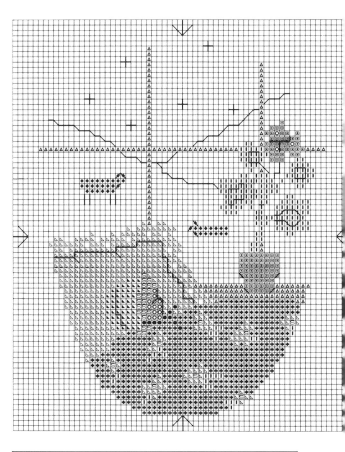

SLEEP BABY, SLEEP ▲

△	white	◣	800 blue
⊃	834 yellow (and stars)	●	798 dark blue
△	3045 ochre	I	3347 green
○	754 flesh (bks eye 3045)		(bks 3052)
✱	3354 pink	◆	3072 grey (bks legs 798)
⊡	3328 red (and bks 3052*)		*Note: one additional backstitch colour**

TWINKLE, TWINKLE ►

◆ white (and bks 793*)
○ 3078 lemon (and eyelet stitch stars)
⊡ 676 yellow
↓ 754 flesh (bks 3354)
✳ 3354 pink (and bks eye)
● 899 red (bks 793)
  *Note: one additional backstitch
  colour*; stitch the eye as shown below:*
| 793 blue (one upright bks eye)

*L*ACE-EDGED CUSHIONS

Pretty and feminine, these lace-edged cushions – made singly or as a pair – will add a touch of luxury and comfort to a young girl's room.

RIDE A COCK-HORSE

Ride a cock-horse to Banbury Cross
To see a fine lady upon a white horse.
With rings on her fingers
And bells on her toes,
She shall have music wherever she goes.

•

LITTLE BO-PEEP

Little Bo-Peep has lost her sheep
And doesn't know where to find them.
Leave them alone,
And they will come home
Wagging their tails behind them.

RIDE A COCK HORSE ▲

○ 743 yellow (bks on saddle blanket)	⊆ 676 gold	◆ 554 lilac (and bks 550*)
‖ white (bks 414)	÷ 948 flesh (bks 352)	l 800 blue
● 745 pale yellow (bks 436) △ gold thread (bks 839)	⊡ 352 pink	↓ 436 light brown (and bks 43)

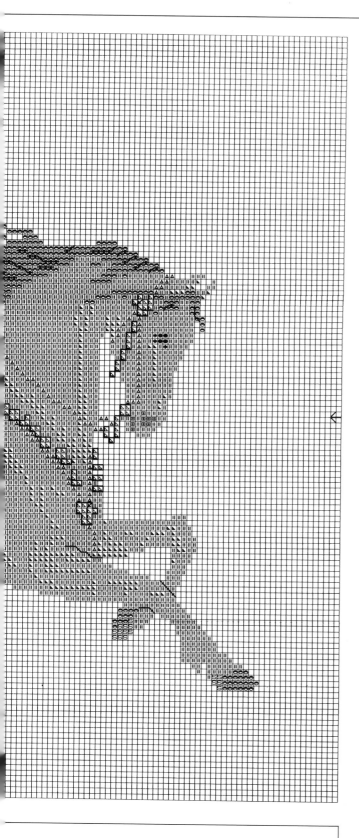

RIDE A COCK-HORSE

YOU WILL NEED

For a cover measuring 35cm (14in) square:

*40cm (16in) square of blue evenweave (Aida)
fabric, 14 threads to 2.5cm (1in)
38cm (15in) square of blue floral print backing
fabric; 12mm (½in) seam allowances are included
150cm (1⅔yds) of white pre-gathered lace trim,
4cm (1½in) wide
DMC stranded embroidery cotton in the colours
given in the panel
No24 tapestry needle
Matching sewing thread
38cm (15in) square cushion pad*

•

THE EMBROIDERY

Following the instructions given on page 121, prepare and stretch your fabric in an embroidery frame. Using two strands of thread in the needle throughout, complete the cross stitching. Work the backstitching on top, using a single strand of thread. Remove the embroidery from the frame, and steam press on the wrong side.

MAKING UP THE CUSHION

Before removing the basting threads, trim the embroidery to measure 38cm (15in) square, using the threads as a guide for measuring and thus keeping the design in the centre of the fabric.

Using a tiny french seam, join the raw edges of the lace together. Baste the edge of the lace to the outer edge, on the right side of the embroidery, placing the bound edge of the lace just inside the 12mm (½in) seam allowance and lying on the fabric. Allow a little extra fullness at the corners. Machine stitch in place.

With right sides together, place the backing fabric on top. Baste and machine stitch around the edges, leaving a 20cm (8in) opening in the middle of one side. Remove the basting; trim across the corners, and turn the cover to the right side. Insert the cushion pad; turn in the edges of the opening, and slipstitch to close.

△ 3064 brown (bks 839)   ● 310 black
✱ 839 dark brown   *Note: 3 additional*
◣ 415 grey (and bks 414*)   *backstitch colours*

LITTLE BO-PEEP ►

- S 676 straw (and bks 780*)
- I 948 flesh (and bks 352*)
- ◣ 927 drab tuquoise (bks 924)
- ● 800 blue
- ↓ 3364 green
- △ 3362 drab green
- ○ 924 dark green (and bks 3371*)
- ⊡ 435 light brown (bks eyebrow)
- ✚ 611 brown
- ◆ 415 grey

Note: 3 additional backstitch colours

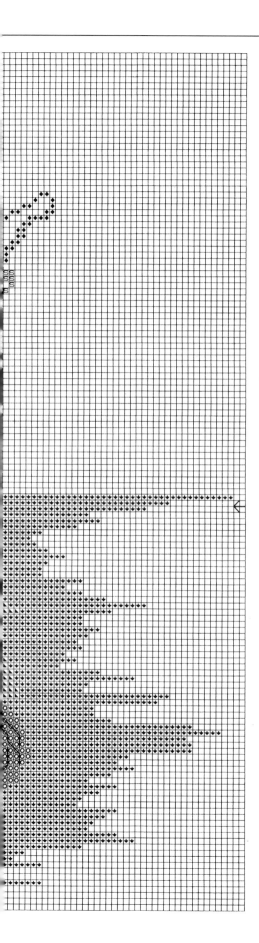

LITTLE BO-PEEP

YOU WILL NEED

For a cushion measuring 35cm (14in) square:

*40cm (16in) square of cream evenweave (Aida)
fabric, 16 threads to 2.5cm (1in)
38cm (15in) square of contrast floral print for
the backing; 12mm (½in) seam allowances
are included
250cm (2⅔yds) of cream lace trim;
4cm (1½in) wide
DMC stranded embroidery cotton in the colours
given in the panel
No 26 tapestry needle
Matching sewing thread
38cm (15in) square cushion pad*

•

THE EMBROIDERY

Prepare the fabric and stretch it in an embroidery frame, following the instructions given on page 121. Referring to the chart, complete the cross stitching, using two strands of thread in the needle. Work the backstitching on top, using a single strand of thread. Take the embroidery out of the frame and steam press it on the wrong side.

MAKING UP THE CUSHION

Trim the embroidery to 38cm (15in) square, as for the Ride a cock-horse cushion, see page 112.

Using a tiny french seam, join the short edges of the lace together. Run a gathering thread close to the straight edge. Pull up the gathers to fit, and with the right side of the embroidery facing and the lace lying on the fabric, baste the edging to the outer edge, placing it just inside the seam allowance. Adjust the gathers evenly, allowing a little extra fullness at the corners. Machine stitch in place.

Place the backing fabric on top, right sides together; baste and machine stitch around, leaving a 20cm (8in) opening in the middle of one side. Take out the basting; trim across the corners, and turn the cover through. Insert the cushion pad and slipstitch the opening to secure.

$\mathscr{A}$LPHABET

A beautifully designed alphabet has many uses in cross stitch embroidery. It can be stitched *en bloc* as a patchwork motif for a child's quilt, for example, or individual letters can be embroidered on separate patches. Alternatively, the letters can be adapted to spell out a greeting on a card or a birth quilt, or incorporated into a design for a

cushion or a small picture to commemorate a special occasion, such as a wedding or a birthday.

Gifts can be personalized by adding initials or a name, or you can even make a traditional alphabet sampler, also utilizing border designs from pages 118 or taking motifs from other projects in this book and repeating them to make patterns.

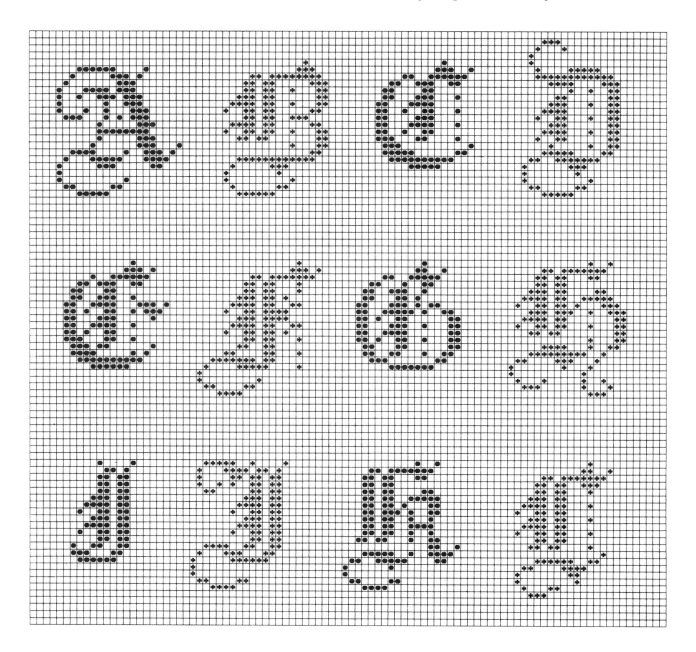

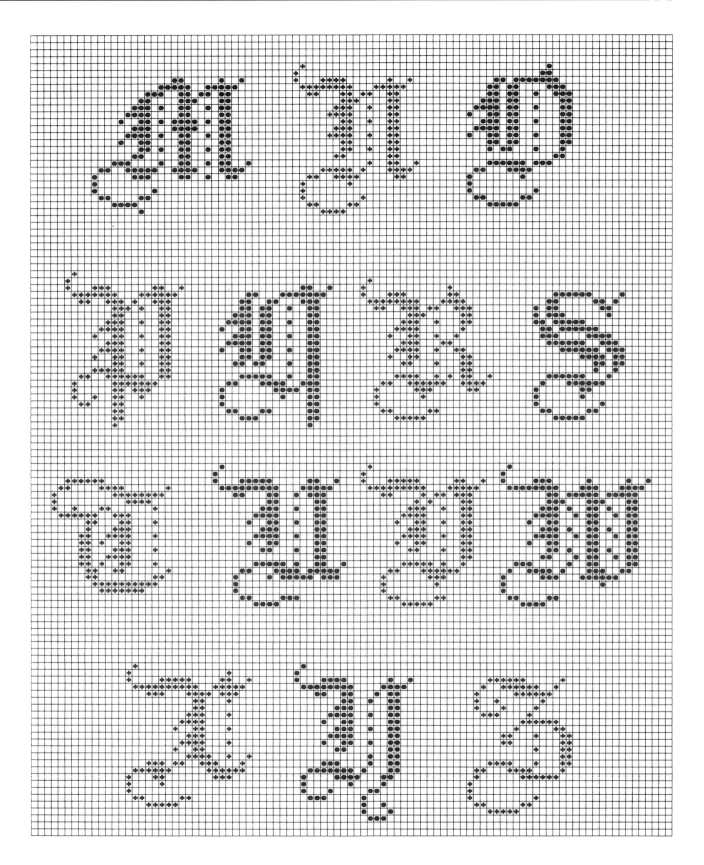

BORDER DESIGNS

A well-chosen border will give a finishing touch to your embroidery that can be as simple or as complex as you like. The selection given here is purely inspirational, but any of these could easily be copied or adapted to suit your own design ideas.

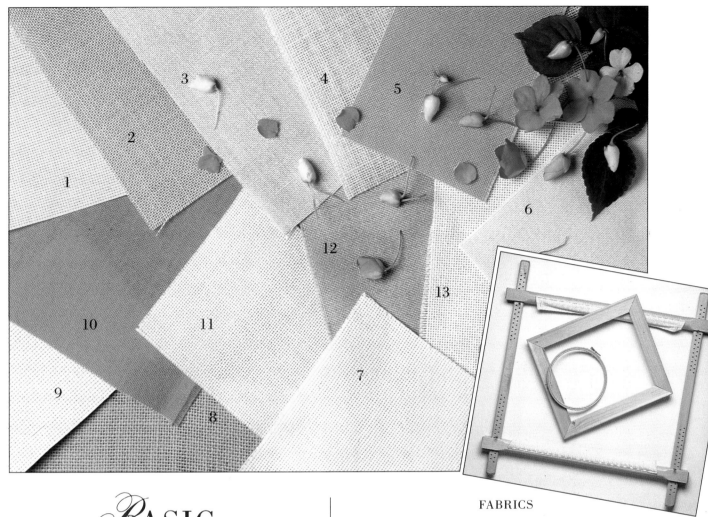

ℬASIC EQUIPMENT

The basic equipment needed for cross stitching is moderately simple and can be bought at most department stores or needlework suppliers. In fact, when you begin to collect the items together, you will probably find that you already have most of them in your workbox and around the home.

*1 16 count Aida; **2** 24ct linen; **3** 30ct linen; **4** 20ct linen; **5** 25ct Linda; **6** 27ct Linda; **7** 16ct Hardanger; **8** 16ct linen; **9** 14ct Aida; **10** 28ct cotton; **11** 18ct wool; **12** 18ct Ainring; **13** 18ct Davosa.*

FABRICS

For best results, cross stitch is worked on an even-weave fabric. This is any fabric with the same number of threads counted in both directions over, for example, 2.5cm (1in).

Traditionally, cross stitch embroidery is worked on linen, which often has a charming hand-woven finish. Although they are not now produced in the variety and quantities of former years and those that are available tend to be expensive, linens in a limited range of weights and colours – including Hardanger and huckaback types – can be brought from specialist suppliers. Whereas ordinary linens have a single weave, Hardanger has a double weave, and huckaback is woven in groups of threads to form a checked pattern.

In addition to linens, many other evenweaves are available, some made from cotton and others from a blend of synthetic and cotton fibres. These fabrics include Zweigart's Aida and Tula, which are woven with groups of threads and have a pronounced checked effect. They are produced in different weights and many colours. Zweigart's Lugana and Linda have a single weave and are also available in a range of weights and colours.

Aida and some other cotton fabrics can be quite stiff to handle, due to the fact that they are finished with a fairly heavy dressing. This will wash out to a certain extent, and although the stiffened fabric will help to give the embroidery an even tension, you may prefer to hand wash the fabric beforehand.

THREADS

Different types of thread can be used for cross stitch embroidery but, for the purposes of this book, stranded embroidery cotton has been used throughout. The number of strands required for each project is given with the instructions. As a general rule, however, the thickness of the embroidery thread should match the weight of the fabric. And for best results, the aim should be to have clearly defined stitches which cover the fabric well and give a sharpness to the overall design.

NEEDLES

For cross stitching on evenweave fabric, use round-ended tapestry needles. You will find that these move easily between the intersections of the fabric without piercing the ground threads. Tapestry needles are available in sizes ranging from 18–26.

When finishing the projects, a selection of sharps is required for hand sewing, and for quilting, either quilting needles or betweens are recommended.

FRAMES

Depending on the size of the embroidery and the amount of cross stitching involved, either a rectangular frame or a hoop of the appropriate size can be used to support the fabric while stitching.

Although a frame is not an absolute essential, there are positive advantages to using one. Firstly, it will keep the fabric evenly stretched and prevent it from becoming distorted. This can easily happen when working with fabric in the hand, especially if the stitch is made by 'scooping' the fabric.

Secondly, if the frame is supported, this leaves both hands free to stitch. With one hand on top and the other below, the correct up and down move-

ments can be used and, with practice, you will find that you can work quicker this way.

SCISSORS

In all fabric crafts it is essential to keep the right type of scissors for the job. For cutting out, use sharp dressmaker's shears and, to prevent the blades from becoming blunt, do not allow them to be used for other tasks. For snipping into seams and cutting threads, a pair of sharp-pointed small embroidery scissors are needed. It is also a good idea to have a pair of general-purpose scissors for cutting paper, card, cord and so on.

SEWING MACHINE

A sewing machine should be used for all making-up purposes where seaming is involved, especially on large items such as quilts and cushion covers. You will not need an elaborate machine to make up the projects in this book. All that is required is that it stitches reliably, gives a good straight stitch and, ideally, has a reverse stitch for convenience when starting and finishing.

IRON

This is one of the most important pieces of equipment required for any fabric craft. A thermostatically controlled steam iron gives excellent results and is particularly good for this type of embroidery, for pressing seams, and for general ironing.

When making up projects, always keep your iron and board to hand so that you can 'press as you sew' to get the very best finish.

GENERAL ACCESSORIES

In addition to the items already mentioned; you will require a good supply of dressmaker's stainless steel pins, a measuring tape, basting thread, ruler and pencil.

While a thimble is not necessarily used for embroidery, it is a good idea to use one for general sewing purposes, especially for hand-sewing through bulky seams. For all kinds of quilting, you will find that one, if not two, thimbles are essential. Here, the second thimble is worn on the first or second finger of the hand that works below the frame as it guides the needle back through the fabric.

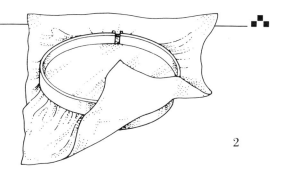

BASIC SKILLS

The basic skills required for making the projects in the book can be found in the following pages.

PREPARING THE FABRIC

Unless fabrics have been stored unfolded on a roll, they will probably be creased, especially along the centre. Before cutting out, therefore, steam press all fabrics to remove any creases. When cutting out main sections, try to be as economical as possible, cutting on the grainline to avoid wastage.

Even with an average amount of handling, many evenweave fabrics tend to fray at the edges, so it is a good idea to overcast the raw edges, using ordinary sewing thread, before embroidering. When calculating quantities, always allow extra fabric to account for the possibility of fraying.

WORKING IN A HOOP

A hoop is the most popular frame for use with small areas of embroidery. It consists of two rings, one fitted inside the other; the outer ring usually has an adjustable screw attachment so that it can be tightened to hold the stretched fabric in place. Hoops are available in several sizes, ranging from 10cm (4in) in diameter to quilting hoops with a diameter of 38cm (15in). Hoops with table stands or floor stands attached are also available.

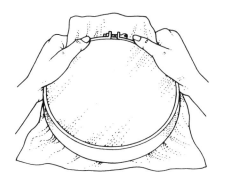

1

1 To stretch your fabric in a hoop, place the area to be embroidered over the inner ring and press the outer ring over it, with the tension screw released.

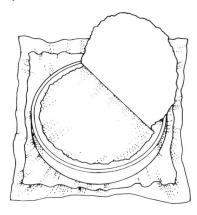

2

2 Smooth the fabric and, if needed, straighten the grain before tightening the screw. The fabric should be evenly stretched.

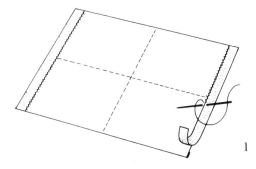

3

3 Tissue paper can be placed between the outer ring and the embroidery, so that the hoop does not mark the fabric. Tear away the paper as shown.

WORKING IN A RECTANGULAR FRAME

Rectangular frames consist of two rollers, with tapes attached, and two flat side pieces, which slot into the rollers and are held in place by pegs or screw attachments. They are measured by the length of the roller tape, and range in size from 30cm (12in) to 68cm (27in). As alternatives to a slate frame, canvas stretchers and the backs of old picture frames can be used.

1

1 To stretch your fabric in a rectangular frame, cut out the fabric, allowing at least an extra 5cm (2in) all around the finished size of the embroidery. Baste a single 12mm (½in) turning on the top and bottom edges and oversew strong tape, 2.5cm (1in) wide, to the other two sides. Mark the centre line both ways with basting stitches.

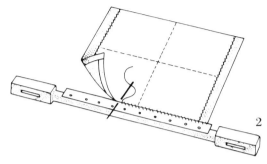

2 Working from the centre outwards and using strong thread, oversew the top and bottom edges to the roller tapes. Fit the side pieces into the slots, and roll any extra fabric on one roller until the fabric is taut.

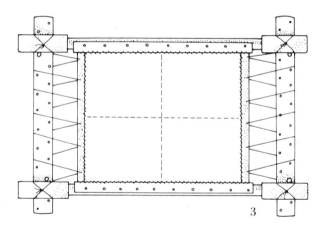

3 Insert the pegs or adjust the screw attachments to secure the frame. Thread a large-eyed needle (chenille needle) with strong thread or fine string and lace both edges, securing the ends around the intersections of the frame. Lace the webbing at 2.5cm (1in) intervals, stretching the fabric evenly.

ENLARGING A GRAPH PATTERN

One or two graph patterns are given in this book. These must be enlarged to the correct size. The scale of the full-size pattern is given on the appropriate page; for example, 'Each square = 5cm (2in)' means that each small square on the printed diagram should correspond to a 5cm (2in) square on your enlarged grid.

1 square = 2.5cm (1in)

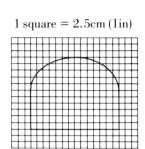 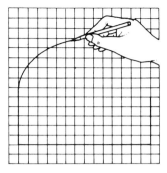

● To enlarge a graph pattern, you will need a sheet of graph paper ruled in 1cm (⅜in) squares, a ruler and pencil. If, for example, the scale is one square to 5cm (2in) you should first mark the appropriate lines to give a grid of the correct size. Copy the graph freehand from the small grid to the larger one, completing one square at a time. Use a ruler to draw the straight lines first, and then copy the freehand curves.

BIAS BINDING

As its name suggests, bias binding is cut across the grain to allow the most 'give', and is an excellent binding for all edges, especially curves.

It is available in three sizes: 12mm (½in), 2.5cm (1in) and 5cm (2in), and in a wonderful variety of colours. Cotton lawn is by far the most popular and practical type, although satins and synthetic mixes are also available. Two methods of binding an edge are shown here; in the first, the binding is attached by stitching through all layers, while in the second it is attached in two stages, so that the stitching cannot be seen on the right side of the fabric.

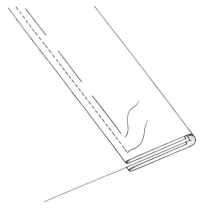

● Using double-fold bias binding, encase the raw edge with binding and baste in place. Working from the right side, machine stitch along the edge so that both sides are stitched at the same time.

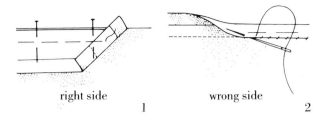

right side   1   wrong side   2

1 Alternatively, open out the turning on one edge of the binding and pin in position on the right side of the fabric, matching the fold to the seamline. Fold over the cut end of the binding. Finish by overlapping the starting point by about 12mm (½in). Pin, baste and machine stitch to cover the seamline.

2 Fold the binding over the raw edge to the wrong side, baste and, using matching sewing thread, neatly hem to finish.

PIPED SEAMS

Contrasting piping adds a special decorative finish to a seam and looks particularly attractive on items such as cushions and cosies.

You can cover piping cord with either bias-cut fabric of your choice or a bias binding; alternatively, ready-covered piping cord is available in several widths and many colours.

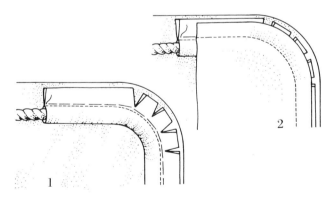

1 To apply piping, pin, baste and stitch it to the right side of the fabric, with seam lines matching. Clip into the seam allowance where necessary.

2 With right sides together, place the second piece of fabric on top, enclosing the piping. Baste and then either hand stitch in place or machine stitch, using a zipper foot. Stitch as close to the piping as possible, covering the first line of stitching.

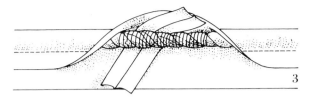

3 To join ends of piping together, first overlap the two ends by about 2.5cm (1in). Unpick the two cut ends of bias to reveal the cord. Join the bias strip as shown. Trim and press the seam open. Unravel the cord, and splice the two ends. Fold the bias strip over the cord, and finish basting around the edge.

MITRING CORNERS

There are several types of mitre, but in each case the purpose is essentially to reduce bulk and to make the corner neat and square.

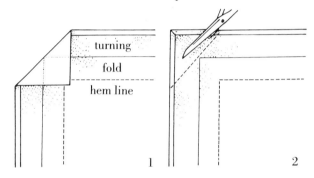

turning

fold

hem line

1   2

1 To mitre a corner, first plan the depth of the hem and allow an extra 6mm (¼in) for turning. Fold over the corner as shown in the diagram and finger-press the creaseline.

2 Allow a further 6mm (¼in) beyond this line and cut across.

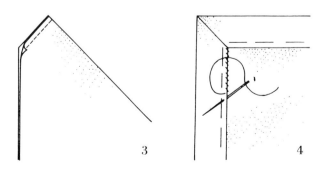

3   4

3 Fold the fabric with the two outer edges together and machine stitch across, taking a 6mm (¼in) seam and stopping at the creased line of the hem.

4 Press the seam open and turn the corner to the right side. Either turn under the hem, baste and hem on the wrong side or, if you are hemstitching, work on the right side, following the instructions given with the project.

ATTACHING A CORD

A twisted cord in plain or mixed colours gives a pretty finish to a cushion. Cords are available in wool, cotton, silk and synthetic fibres and in a great variety of colours and thicknesses.

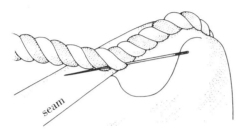

● To attach a cord, simply slip one cut end into the seam and secure with matching thread. Slipstitch the cord around the edge of the cushion, alternately catching the underside of the cord only and sliding the needle under the seam so that the finished stitching is completely hidden.
Finish with the two ends just overlapped, neatly tucked into the seam and firmly secured.

MOUNTING EMBROIDERY

Embroidered pictures and other similar projects look best if they are first stretched over cardboard before framing. Very lightweight fabrics can be attached at the back with pieces of masking tape, but heavier fabrics are best laced across the back.

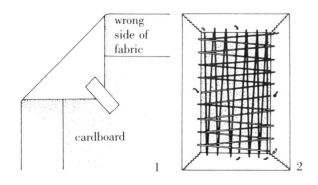

1 The cardboard should be cut to the size of the finished embroidery, with an extra 6mm (¼in)

added all around to allow for the recess in the picture frame.

2 With the embroidery face down and the cardboard centred over it, fold over the edges of the fabric on opposite sides and lace across, using strong thread. Repeat on the other two sides, first folding each corner into a mitre. Finally, pull up the stitches fairly tightly to stretch the fabric firmly over the cardboard. Overstitch the mitred corners.

SEAMS

Unless otherwise stated, all seams are straight seams, with a 12mm (½in) seam allowance, pressed open to finish. In some cases, a french seam is specified. To make this, place the two fabrics with wrong sides together and join them with a narrow seam. Press the seam to one side, and turn the two pieces so that the wrong sides are now facing outwards. Make a second seam enclosing the first.

CROSS STITCH

For all cross stitch embroidery, the following two methods of working are used. In each case, neat rows of vertical stitches are produced on the back of the fabric.

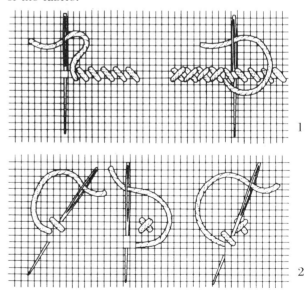

1 When stitching large areas, work in horizontal rows. Working from right to left, complete the first row of evenly spaced diagonal stitches over the number of threads specified in the project instructions. Then, working from left to right, repeat the process. Continue in this way, making sure each stitch and successive rows cross in the same direction throughout.

2 When stitching diagonal lines, work downwards, completing each stitch before moving to the next.

HEMSTITCH

This stitch is the traditional way of finishing the hems of embroidered napkins and tablecloths. For a fringed hem, remove a single thread at the hem and stitch along the line as shown. When you have finished, remove the weft threads below the hemstitching, to make a fringe.

To secure a hem that has been turned up to the drawn-thread line and basted, hemstitch as shown, but at the second stage of each stitch ensure that the needle pierces the hem at the back of the fabric before you pull the thread through, ready to repeat the stitch along the line.

Note When hemstitching Aida and similar fabrics, it is not necessary to remove the initial thread, as the lines between blocks are clearly distinguished; the stitches can be worked along a line of blocks or groups of threads. As you are stitching blocks instead of single threads, make sure that you refer to the project instructions to discover the number of blocks to work for the hemstitching.

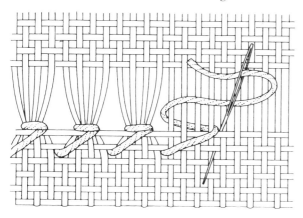

Bring the needle out on the right side, two threads below the drawn-thread line. Working from left to right, pick up either two or three threads, as shown in the diagram. Bring the needle out again and insert it behind the fabric, to emerge two threads down, ready to make the next stitch. Before reinserting the needle, pull the thread tight, so that the bound threads form a neat group.

BACKSTITCH

Backstitch is used in the projects to give emphasis to a particular foldline, an outline or a shadow. The stitches are worked over the same number of threads as the cross stitch, forming continuous straight or diagonal lines.

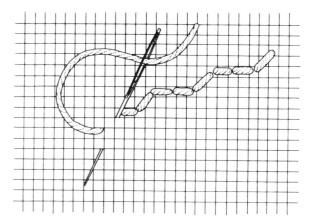

● Make the first stitch from left to right; pass the needle behind the fabric, and bring it out one stitch length ahead to the left. Repeat and continue in this way along the line.

STAR EYELET

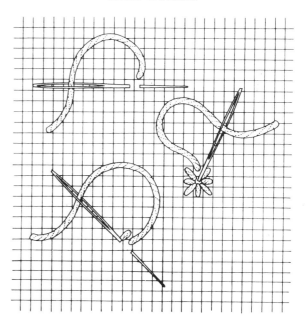

Beginning at the top right corner, work eight straight stitches over two threads (the length of the particular cross stitch being worked), working from the outer edge into the centre, as shown in the diagram.

125

CONVERSION CHART

Not all of these colour conversions are exact matches, and bracketed
numbers are given as close substitutes.

DMC	ANCHOR	COATS	MADERIA	DMC	ANCHOR	COATS	MADERIA	DMC	ANCHOR	COATS	MADERIA
White	2	1001	White	434	309	5000	2009	721	(324)	2329	0308
208	(110)	4301	0804	435	(365)	5371	2010	722	(323)	2099	0307
209	105	4302	0803	436	(363)	5943	2011	725	(306)	2298	0108
210	104	4303	0802	437	362	5942	2012	726	295	2294	0109
213	895	—	0812	444	291	2298	0108	727	293	—	0110
221	(897)	3242	0811	445	288	—	0103	734	(279)	—	1610
224	893	3241	0813	469	267	—	1503	738	942	5375	2013
225	892	3006	0814	471	(280)	—	1501	739	(366)	5369	2014
300	(352)	—	2304	498	(47)	—	0511	740	316	2099	0202
301	(349)	—	2306	517	(162)	—	1107	741	304	2314	0201
304	(47)	3401	0509	535	(401)	8400	1809	742	303	2303	0114
307	(289)	2290	0104	550	(101)	4107	0714	743	(297)	2302	0113
309	(42)	3284	0507	552	100	4092	0713	744	(301)	2293	0112
310	403	8403	Black	553	98	4097	0712	745	(300)	2296	0111
311	148	—	1006	554	(96)	4104	0711	746	(386)	—	0101
312	(147)	7979	1005	564	203	—	1208	754	(6)	2331	0305
317	(400)	8512	1714	597	(168)	—	1110	758	868	2337	0403
318	(399)	8511	1802	602	(63)	3063	0702	760	(9)	3069	0405
319	(246)	6246	1313	603	(62)	3001	0701	761	(8)	3068	0404
320	(216)	6017	1311	605	(50)	3151	0613	762	397	8510	1804
321	47	3500	0510	606	335	2334	0209	772	(264)	6250	1604
322	(978)	7978	1004	608	(333)	2332	0206	776	(24)	3281	0503
326	(59)	3401	0508	610	906	—	2106	778	(968)	—	0808
333	119	—	0903	611	898	—	2107	780	309	—	2214
334	161	7977	1003	612	832	—	2108	781	308	—	2213
335	(42)	3283	0506	613	831	—	2109	782	307	—	2212
340	118	7110	0902	632	(936)	—	2311	783	307	—	2211
341	117	—	0901	640	903	5393	1905	791	941	—	0904
347	(19)	3013	0407	642	392	—	1906	792	941	7150	0905
349	13	2335	0212	644	830	8501	1907	793	121	721	0906
350	(11)	3011	0213	645	(400)	8500	1811	794	120	—	0907
351	(10)	3012	0214	647	(8581)	8900	1813	796	(133)	7100	0913
352	(9)	3008	0303	648	900	8390	1814	797	(132)	7023	0912
353	(8)	3006	0304	666	46	3046	0210	798	(131)	7022	0911
355	5968	2339	0401	676	891	2305	2208	799	(130)	7030	0910
367	(262)	6018	1312	677	(886)	2300	2207	800	(128)	—	0908
368	(261)	6016	1310	680	901	5374	2210	801	(357)	5475	2007
371	(856)	—	2111	699	(923)	6228	1303	806	(169)	—	1108
402	(347)	—	2307	700	229	6227	1304	807	(168)	—	1109
407	(882)	—	2310	701	227	6226	1305	809	(130)	7021	0909
413	401	8514	1713	702	226	6239	1306	813	(160)	—	1013
414	(400)	8513	1801	703	238	6238	1307	814	(44)	—	0514
415	398	8510	1803	704	(256)	6238	1308	815	43	3000	0513
420	(375)	5374	2104	712	(387)	5387	2101	816	(20)	3410	0512
422	(373)	5372	2102	718	88	—	0707	817	47	2335	0211
433	(371)	5471	2008	720	(326)	—	0309	818	48	3281	0502

DMC	ANCHOR	COATS	MADERIA	DMC	ANCHOR	COATS	MADERIA	DMC	ANCHOR	COATS	MADERIA
819	(892)	3280	0501	943	188	—	1203	3078	292	2292	0102
822	(390)	5387	1908	945	881	—	2313	3325	(159)	7976	1002
823	150	—	1008	946	332	—	0207	3326	(26)	3126	0504
824	(164)	—	1010	947	(330)	2327	0205	3328	(11)	3071	0408
825	(162)	—	1011	948	(778)	2331	0306	3345	(268)	6258	1406
826	(161)	—	1012	950	4146	—	2309	3346	(257)	6258	1407
827	(159)	—	1014	951	(880)	—	2308	3347	(267)	6266	1408
828	(158)	—	1101	954	204	—	1211	3348	265	6266	1409
829	(906)	—	2113	955	203	—	1210	3350	69	—	0603
833	907	—	2114	956	54	—	0611	3354	(75)	—	0608
834	874	—	2204	957	52	—	0612	3364	(843)	6010	1603
838	380	7982	1914	958	187	6186	1114	3371	382	—	2004
840	(379)	5379	1912	959	186	6185	1113	3607	(87)	—	0708
841	(378)	5376	1911	961	40	—	0610	3608	86	—	0709
842	376	—	1910	962	52	—	0609	3609	(85)	—	0710
844	401	—	1810	963	48	—	0608	3685	(70)	—	0602
869	(944)	—	2105	966	206	—	1209	3687	(68)	—	0604
890	(218)	6021	1314	970	(316)	2327	0204	3688	(66)	—	0605
891	29	—	0411	971	(316)	2099	0203	3689	73	—	0607
892	28	—	0412	972	303	—	0107	3705	(35)	—	0410
893	27	—	0413	973	297	—	0105	3706	(33)	—	0409
894	26	—	0414	975	352	—	2303	3708	(31)	—	0408
898	360	5476	2006	976	(309)	—	2302	3712	10	—	—
899	(27)	3282	0505	977	(307)	2306	2301	3731	76	—	—
902	(72)	3083	0601	986	(246)	6021	1404	3733	75	—	—
904	(258)	6258	1413	987	(245)	6258	1403	3756	158	—	—
906	(256)	6256	1411	988	(257)	6258	1402	3761	159	—	—
910	(228)	6031	1301	989	(256)	6266	1401	3766	167	—	—
911	(205)	6205	1214	991	212	—	1204	3774	778	—	—
912	209	6225	1212	992	(187)	6186	1202	3779	4146	—	—
919	(341)	2326	0314	993	(186)	—	1201				
920	(339)	3337	0312	995	410	7010	1102				
921	(338)	2326	0311	996	433	7001	1103				
922	(324)	3336	0310	3011	856	—	1607				
924	(851)	6008	1706	3021	(382)	5395	1904				
926	(779)	6007	1707	3022	(8581)	—	1903				
927	(849)	6006	1708	3024	(391)	8390	1901				
928	(900)	7225	1709	3031	(905)	5472	2003				
930	(922)	7052	1712	3033	387	—	2001				
931	(921)	7051	1711	3042	869	4221	0807				
932	(920)	7050	1710	3045	(888)	—	2103				
935	862	—	1505	3046	(887)	2410	2206				
936	269	—	1507	3047	(886)	2300	2205				
937	268	—	1504	3051	(846)	—	1508				
938	381	—	2005	3052	(844)	—	1509				
939	152	—	1009	3053	(859)	6315	1510				

INDEX

SUPPLIERS

The following mail order companies
have supplied some of the basic items
needed for making up the projects in
this book:

United Kingdom
Remember When
Cheriton Cottage
Wreningham
Norwich NR16 1BE. England.

Framecraft Miniatures Limited
148-150 High Street
Aston
Birmingham B6 4US. England.
Telephone (021) 359 4442

Addresses for Framecraft worldwide
Ireland Needlecraft Pty. Ltd.
2-4 Keppel Drive
Hallam
Victoria 3803
Australia

Danish Art Needlework
PO Box 442
Lethbridge
Alberta T1J 3Z1
Canada

Sanyei Imports
PO Box 5
Hashima Shi
Gifu 501-62
Japan

The Embroidery Shop
286 Queen Street
Masterton
New Zealand

Anne Brinkley Designs Inc.
246 Walnut Street
Newton
Mass. 02160
USA

S A Threads and Cottons Ltd.
43 Somerset Road
Cape Town
South Africa